The Doctor Who Sat for a Year

—

BRENDAN KELLY

Marino Branch
Brainse Marino
Tel: 8336297

GILL BOOKS

Gill Books
Hume Avenue
Park West
Dublin 12
www.gillbooks.ie

Gill Books is an imprint of M.H. Gill and Co.

© Brendan Kelly 2019
978 07171 8457 6

Print origination and illustrations by www.grahamthew.com
Copy-edited by Djinn von Noorden
Proofread by Jane Rogers
Printed by CPI Group (UK) Ltd, Croydon CRO4YY

This book is typeset in 11 on 16pt Alegreya Regular.

A CIP catalogue record for this book is available from the British
Library.

5 4 3 2 1

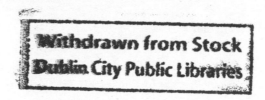
Note

—

This book is intended as general guidance only and does
not in any way represent medical advice for individual
persons. Readers are advised to attend their own healthcare professionals for advice and guidance appropriate
to their particular needs. This book does not in any way
replace the advice and guidance that your own doctor
or other healthcare professional can give you. If you
are concerned about any of the issues raised in this
book, be sure to consult your GP. While every effort has
been made to ensure the accuracy of the information
and material contained in this book, it is still possible
that errors or omissions may occur in the content. The
author and publishers assume no responsibility for,
and give no guarantees or warranties concerning, the
accuracy, completeness or up-to-date nature of the
information provided in this book. Case histories and
names presented in this book are entirely fictional.
They demonstrate common features of certain mental
illnesses but are not based on real people.

About the Author
—

Brendan Kelly is Professor of Psychiatry at Trinity College Dublin, Ireland and Consultant Psychiatrist at Tallaght University Hospital. In addition to his medical degree, Brendan holds master's degrees in epidemiology, healthcare management and Buddhist studies; and doctorates in medicine, history, governance and law. Brendan has authored and co-authored over 250 peer-reviewed publications, 500 non-peer-reviewed publications, 13 book chapters and 11 books, chiefly on themes related to mental health and wellness, most recently *Mental Health in Ireland: The Complete Guide for Patients, Families, Health Care Professionals and Everyone Who Wants To Be Well*.

Contents

This book is dedicated to Regina, Eoin and Isabel

—

PROLOGUE: JUST SIT

—

I am sitting in a beautiful, high-ceilinged room, filled with light.

To be clear: it is the room that is filled with light, not me.

When I shut my eyes twenty minutes ago, there were two other people in the room. More have joined since we started to meditate but I do not know how many. All are quiet, breathing. Outside, cars and buses drive along the street. Passers-by talk and laugh. And then they pass by. So do cars, buses and everything else. They are soon replaced by others. And they too pass.

The room is sparsely furnished and painted white, with large windows facing onto the street at the front and onto a small garden at the back.

All the while, I sit in meditation position, trying to focus on my breath.

I've come to a meditation centre in Dublin city centre early this morning to join an hour-long silent meditation sit. It is perfect. There is no doctrine, no teaching, no talking. Just a few gentle hellos at the start and quiet, friendly goodbyes as we finish.

The silence is not oppressive. It is a gentle, profound silence. The kind of silence that makes you want to be silent, not the kind that makes you want to talk.

I have dropped into these morning meditation sessions infrequently and irregularly over the years. I have not been here for the past year. The sessions are held on weekday mornings and mostly I am at work

1

early so I am unable to attend. And if I am not in work, this part of the morning is the best time for getting other things done, so coming to these sessions is quite a difficult and unlikely decision for me.

But in the context of a week off from work, here I am. And I now remember why I used to come. This is a lovely environment for meditating. Just being in the presence of others, even people I barely know, really adds something to the experience. The hour passes very quickly, even though my thoughts wander repeatedly and I continually need to refocus my mind back onto my breathing.

It is astonishingly simple and astonishingly difficult.

At the end of the hour we quietly put away the mats and cushions, bid each other farewell and slip out into the sunlight.

The outside world is loud, but not unpleasantly so.

INTRODUCTION: WHY MEDITATE?

—

I am a recidivist meditator. Over many years I have attended sporadic meditation classes, joined contemplative groups, undertaken courses, visited the occasional retreat centre, and – like many people – purchased a small mountain of books about meditation, mindfulness and Buddhism. I've even read some of these books and profited to a certain extent from their wisdom. I also have a long-standing interest in Asian cultures, having visited Japan twice and spent a month in China over a decade ago. And, in late 2016, I made a trip to Bangalore in India, spending much of the time happily lost in Hindu temples. And yet meditation has never taken a real root in my life. I have always lacked the discipline to establish a daily meditation practice despite an oddly enduring belief that this would be a good thing to do.

There is much evidence to support my belief in meditation. As a psychiatrist, a medical doctor who treats people with mental illness and psychological problems, I am only too aware of the usefulness of mindfulness in preventing relapse in depression and assisting people with day-to-day psychological problems: anxiety, depression, phobias. I am also mindful (as it were) of the commodification and oversimplification of mindfulness – McMindfulness, if you like. I know full well that people's problems are rarely so straightforward that any single technique, such as mindfulness or meditation, can offer all the answers.

And yet, despite my remarkably consistent failure to meditate, despite my realistic attitude to what meditation can achieve and despite the many other matters clamouring for my attention, I retain the stubborn belief that regular meditation has a great deal to offer.

It is surely no coincidence that virtually all spiritual traditions on the planet incorporate meditative or contemplative practices of various kinds, generally centred on focusing the mind, stilling the thoughts and abiding in a state of reflectiveness and calm. These ancient spiritual practices overlap hugely with modern psychological therapies that are commonly centred on cultivating a steady, non-anxious presence, a deepened awareness of the present moment and an ability to *just sit*. There must be something in this.

With all of this in mind, and with more than a little ambition, I asked myself, late in 2016, whether it was possible, with some dedication and sustained effort, to meditate daily for a year and, if so – would it do me any good?

As a psychiatrist, working full-time and living with my family in Dublin's city centre, I, like so many others, consider myself a busy person. Would it be possible to carve out even a very modest amount of time every day to meditate, over the course of a full year? Would all of the complexities and complications of modern working and family life permit me to meditate for fifteen minutes each day, and record my progress (if any) in this journal?

For better or for worse I decided to try, and that is how this book was born.

At the start I gave myself a 10 per cent chance of completing the project: a year is a *very* long time. But as I got into it, my project became something a little different from what I had planned: more diffuse, more reflective, more self-sustaining. There was less meditation than I would have liked and more self-reflection than I might have predicted. And there was a phenomenal amount of chatter about random topics that came lolloping into my poor addled brain at every opportunity.

But none of this was predictable at the start and all of it will unfold in the pages that lie ahead. At the start, my project was fundamentally, clearly and simply rooted in my interest in meditation and, especially, my long-standing fascination with Buddhism.

The Story of Buddha

Today meditation is most commonly associated with Buddhist tradition, which has always been of great interest to me. But despite reading about Buddhism for many years, I remain puzzled by Buddhism's central story, the life story of the Buddha himself.

According to traditional accounts, Siddhārtha Gautama was born in northeast India around 566 BC. His father was a local chieftain and, warned of his son's tendency towards asceticism, provided Siddhārtha with a very protected upbringing whereby Siddhārtha would not have to confront the realities of age, sickness and death until he was older. At the age of sixteen Siddhārtha married Yasodhara, a beautiful princess, and soon they had a son.

At a certain point Siddhārtha became dissatisfied with his life of privilege and left his home to become a wandering ascetic or *śramana*. While Siddhārtha did not leave his wife and child in an impoverished or unsupported setting, he still just walked out on them in the classic fashion of a deadbeat dad. That does not seem like an especially compassionate or enlightened act, surely?

Anyway, after several years of meditation and self-mortification, Siddhārtha still felt unfulfilled and went to meditate further beneath a sacred bodhi tree in Bodhgaya, northeast India, vowing that he would die beneath that tree rather than arise without the wisdom he sought. Siddhārtha was subjected to several forms of temptation and attack, but resisted stoutly and continued meditating. Some time later, during a night of meditation, Siddhārtha attained enlightenment, passing through several stages of illumination, culminating with him finally seeing the exact condition of all living beings and perceiving the cause and solution to suffering. At this point Siddhārtha became a 'Buddha' or awakened one.

It all makes for a pretty compelling story, and Buddha went on to deliver inspiring teachings of great gentleness and power, centred on kindness and compassion, stillness and insight. And it is the content and tone of these teachings that leave me even more puzzled about why Siddhārtha left his wife and child in order to pursue his path. I understand that he wished to renounce worldly things so as to focus on the search for truth, that he didn't leave his family without means or support and that society was probably very different then.

But simply walking out on his wife and child still seems to me like an unwise, unskilful move, lacking in compassion. Surely there was a better, less hurtful way? And surely today there are less dramatic, more sustainable ways to pursue a contemplative path?

In many ways, that is precisely what this book is about.

The Structure of this Book

This story in this book is considerably less dramatic than the story of Buddha. But, inspired by Buddhist tradition, as I go through my own meditation project I have used the central tenets of Buddhist thought to structure my journal and to provide an overview of the philosophy and psychology underpinning Buddhist practices.

With this in mind I use the most important aspects of Buddhist tradition, the 'four noble truths' and 'the noble eightfold path' to inform each month of my year-long project. In thinking about these teachings it is important to note that Buddhist teaching is at once a philosophy, a psychology and an ethics; that is, Buddhist teaching provides a specific system or set of beliefs about reality (philosophy), a specific theory of the human mind and human behaviour (psychology) and a specific set of recommendations for appropriate conduct (ethics). All three are mixed together in Buddhism: philosophy, psychology and ethics.

The four noble truths are centrally concerned with human suffering (*duhkha*) and the way to overcome suffering. During the first four months of my meditation journal (January to April 2017), I focus on each of these noble truths in turn, starting with the first, which is *duhkha* itself. *Duhkha* is often translated as 'suffering' though it can also mean 'pain' or 'unease'. In essence, it refers to the unsatisfactoriness of much of human experience and behaviour and points to a need to identify the root cause of *duhkha* and overcome it.

The second noble truth (discussed in February) is the causes of *duhkha*, which, in Buddhist tradition, are craving (also translated as 'grasping' or 'attachment'), hatred and delusion. These experiences are most often embedded in our responses to sensory phenomena and the world around us, and this truth provides much of the basis for Buddhism's focus on the practice of meditation as a key way to attain calmness, improve insight and move towards enlightenment.

The third noble truth (discussed in March) is the cessation of suffering, which we can achieve by facing *duhkha* and overcoming craving, aversion and delusion. This is the ultimate aim of Buddhist practice and is known as *nirvana* or *nibbana*. Finally, the fourth noble truth (discussed in April) is *how* to overcome *duhkha* through the noble eightfold path, based on the three key principles of wisdom, moral virtue and meditation.

The noble eightfold path is a set of guidelines about how best to think and behave in the world in order to reduce suffering. The eight elements of the path are:

- right view (*discussed in May*)
- right resolve (*June*)
- right speech (*July*)
- right action (*August*)
- right livelihood (*September*)
- right effort (*October*)
- right mindfulness (*November*)
- right concentration (*December*).

I touch on each of these themes in turn as my journal unfolds and, as with the four noble truths, the Buddhist canon contains many more detailed accounts of the noble eightfold path for those who seek further information. The final month in my journal, January 2018, reflects on what, if anything, my year-long meditation project has achieved. As I write these words, I have no idea what that chapter will contain, if anything.

Throughout the journal, I touch on many specific themes in passing and, in order to provide more information on some of them, I include essays on key topics ranging from the usefulness of meditation for maintaining mental health to guidance about mindfulness in the challenging setting of budget airlines. These additional essays and other relevant publications are mentioned at various points throughout the journal as they came to the fore in my thinking. Relevant bibliographic details are provided in the references section. There is also a concluding chapter on how to meditate.

Finally, it is important to note that this is a *meditation* journal focused on meditation practice rather than anything else. The story also touches on how meditation affected me in my work as a psychiatrist – other aspects of my life, such as family, friends and other activities, feature only to the extent that they are relevant to the meditation project. They were, however, always going on in the background. In addition to what you read here there were very many other things happening too – far too many to mention.

And it is, perhaps, this busy-ness, too complex and intense to record in any journal, that makes meditation essential, now more than ever.

Sometimes it's good to just sit.

'Don't just do something. Sit there.'

—

Buddhist proverb

THE FOUR NOBLE TRUTHS

—

January

—

EVERYTHING IS UNSATISFACTORY

In which I try to establish an embarrassingly modest meditation habit and encounter all of the challenges described in the many unopened meditation handbooks piled by my bedside. I realise how distracted I am during most of my daily activities but continue with all of them anyway. Despite everything, and for reasons I cannot fathom, I do not abandon my meditation project.

Sunday 1 January

I sit on the floor in the living room at 7 am on New Year's Day. The morning is chilly but pleasantly so. The Christmas tree is fragrant and atmospheric: Christmas is far from over in this house. I am happy I had an early night last night. I must have slept straight through any fireworks or celebrations outside. I am rested and, for once, entirely ready for the new year. I sit.

I focus on my breath. I count gently on the intake of breath for ten breaths. I count gently on the turning of the breath for ten breaths. I count gently on the out breath for ten breaths. I try to be mindful, in the moment.

I hear birds outside the window and my thoughts wander. This is good, I think. This is the point of the exercise. My thoughts need to wander so that I can bring them back to my breath. This is the work of meditation. My head needs to fill with a million pointless thoughts so that I can let them pass and focus on the present moment.

I still hear the birds. They aren't going away. They sound very happy. And they aren't meditating, I presume. Or are they? Maybe they're singing *mindfully*? If they are, I bet they're a lot less agonised about it than I am.

I am trying to meditate every day for the next year, starting with just ten to fifteen minutes per day for the first month. How hard can it be? This is day one.

–

Monday 2 January

I am in the kitchen at 6.30 in the morning trying to focus on my breath again. I am fortunate to be a habitual early riser: I have no need for an alarm clock to wake me up. To find time to meditate, I simply re-allocate this first part of the day from reading or computer work to sitting and focusing on my breath. But today this proves utterly impossible. Disaster! And it is only day two.

While I should be meditating, I keep thinking about what I will be doing later today: taking Italian visitors around Dublin and visiting

Newgrange. I banish these thoughts and try to focus on the intake of my breath. No luck. I keep thinking about the pantomime I saw yesterday at the Gaiety, *Robin Hood and his Merry Men*. It was excellent. The actors were so energetic and absorbed in the performance; perhaps that is a form of mindfulness for them – complete absorption in the present moment.

I banish this thought and try again to focus on my breath. No luck. Perhaps I should have decided to go for a run each morning instead of meditating. Am I being lazy? I banish this thought too and try to return to my breath. No luck again: what I will write in this journal? Perhaps keeping a journal is a mistake, another distraction, another way to avoid real, plain, simple, unvarnished, un-intellectualised meditation? I resolve to write about these distracting thoughts and how I banished them, then spend some time thinking about what, precisely, I will write about banishing my distracting thoughts ...

As I wearily banish these thoughts too, my phone makes a sound like wind chimes. Ten minutes have elapsed. Time's up for today. And still I am not enlightened. I have not yet levitated but that, surely, is entirely reasonable? Twenty minutes of bad meditation over two days cannot possibly be enough.

Still and all, perhaps yesterday's happy birds know something I don't. They are outside the window again today, still singing their hearts out and they still sound very happy. In contrast, I am irritated.

–

Tuesday 3 January

I am back at work after the Christmas break. Yesterday we took our Italian visitors to Newgrange. Last year I was lucky enough to visit the monument at dawn during the winter solstice days when the rising sun beams into the chamber, its ancient light bringing the promise of spring. Yesterday the tour guide drifted into an odd, misty, quasi-mystical state as he speculated about the possible meaning of the monument. It is, admittedly, a very spiritual place, set atop a hill overlooking beautiful countryside.

Newgrange would be a splendid spot for meditation were it not for the thousands of people marching past; the school tours, the tour guides and the endless buses. Perhaps if one came here in the early morning it would be quieter, or if one was a more accomplished meditator one could simply transcend these distractions. But not me: I'm on day three of my year-long meditation project so I scarcely count as experienced. At least not yet.

Nonetheless, I meditate for an endless, distracted ten minutes today, sitting quietly in a chair. I'm baffled that anyone can fall asleep while trying to meditate yet I've seen it happen many times during my episodic attendances at meditation classes over the years. How can it be? When I try to meditate my mind hops madly about the place, like a monkey in a tree, swinging to and fro, chattering endlessly, babbling inanely. I must try to let it settle.

–

Wednesday 4 January
Does it matter where I meditate? Goodness, yes. Meditating in my office before work is dreadful, distracting and frustrating. My head is filled with important work-related thoughts that I feel I must write down, but I resist. And then, after ten extremely unpleasant minutes 'meditating', I forget them all. Maybe they really were genuinely important thoughts? It does not matter: they are gone now. And so is the person who thought them, because Buddhism teaches that the 'self' changes so quickly it is misleading to think of a constant fixed self at all. The world is in constant flux, everything changes, and, most of all, the self changes at the speed of light.

And thank goodness for that. Today's self meditated poorly. Perhaps tomorrow's self will do better. I just need to keep on trying. In the past I found that additional supports – meditative music, earplugs, special chairs – serve only as distractions. Simplicity and focus are key and tomorrow I will try again.

Thursday 5 January

I travel to Paris for a meeting tomorrow, working busily on my computer at the airport in the early morning and on the plane. In the late afternoon I visit the Musée Guimet, a glorious Parisian museum of Asian art with tens of thousands of pieces from seventeen Asian countries. I came upon it by chance many years ago and seek it out again on this trip. Just up the street from the main museum the Galeries du Panthéon Bouddhique contain an especially astonishing collection of Buddhist art, with hundreds of Buddha figures. They are all meditating serenely, unlike me.

Appropriately inspired, I meditate in splendid solitude for a good fifteen minutes in my hotel room on the Avenue Édouard-Vaillant. This is my best meditation day so far this year by a very long shot. Quiet, undisturbed, undistracted.

But do I need to travel to Paris every time I want to meditate? Perhaps I do, but there is no point worrying about this now: progress is progress and I should be thankful. That is more than enough for the time being. And so, to bed.

–

Friday 6 January

To the irritation of many, I have always been a morning person. At around 6 am every day I sit bolt upright, fully awake, 100 per cent ready for the day. Morning is the best time for everything: work, exercise, meditating. I think carefully about how to spend these early morning hours because the rest of my day usually gets busier and distractions become ubiquitous. Waking up to a crisp Paris morning, I work for a couple of hours, meditate for fifteen peaceful minutes, and then take a walk in the Jardin des Tuileries. The garden is quiet and elegant, crisp and cool. It is unutterably serene. This is the Paris I love.

My meeting begins later that morning. I eat snails at lunchtime but they are so comprehensively smothered in garlic that I've no idea what they taste like. No matter. I am not an enthusiast of French cuisine at the best of times. I prefer Asian food. In the evening, I have dinner alone in a pleasantly anonymous, weirdly quiet hotel restaurant, reading a magazine article about silence. I wonder would the magazine have been better off omitting the text of the article and simply printing three blank pages, advising readers to sit silently with their eyes shut for fifteen minutes, rather than reading about silence?

—

Saturday 7 January

This month's theme is *duhkha*, the first of the four noble truths of Buddhism. *Duhkha* is often translated as 'suffering', although it can also mean 'pain' or 'unease'. In essence, *duhkha* refers to the ultimate unsatisfactoriness of much of human experience and behaviour, and points to a need to identify the root cause of *duhkha* and to overcome it.

I think of *duhkha* as unsatisfactoriness rather than suffering because I readily identify with the idea that everything in life is in some way unsatisfying. And, as a privileged resident of a rich, developed country (Ireland), it would be wrong to describe my day-to-day travails as 'suffering'. Besides, unsatisfactoriness is much closer to the original meaning of the Buddhist term.

Waking up on my final morning in magical, magical Paris, I still manage to find unsatisfactoriness all around. Perhaps I have some kind of gift for finding *duhkha* even in the most amazing locations. For example, it feels unsatisfactory that this is my final morning in Paris, a city I love (French cuisine notwithstanding). This is entirely ridiculous: I've had a good trip, my work meeting went well and I can revisit the Musée Guimet this morning to gaze at Asian art as I'm heading home to my incredibly privileged life in the middle of a weekend off work. I have absolutely nothing to complain about.

And yet feelings of unsatisfactoriness lurk all around. *Duhkha* is everywhere. I meditate (unsatisfactorily) for fifteen minutes in my hotel room before working for a couple of hours, visiting the Sorbonne briefly and travelling (satisfactorily) back to Dublin.

Just to be clear: I love Paris.

Sunday 8 January

The day is dominated by activities relating to a book I wrote recently, *Hearing Voices*. I have devoted a great deal of time to this book over the past three years, exploring the history of psychiatry in Ireland from earliest times to the present day and appealing for better health and social services for the mentally ill. There is a positive review in a national newspaper and I record an interview for *The History Show* on RTÉ Radio 1.

Before all of this, in the early morning, I sit for fifteen minutes, trying to meditate. I know there is a book review appearing later in the day and I try – with moderate success – to set aside my curiosity and anxiety and to focus on my breathing. To complicate matters, the cat, Trixie, sits gazing at me, unblinking, as I meditate. Trixie is a lovely, friendly creature, white with black patches and as curious as she is patient. She is utterly accepting of whatever life brings her. Right now Trixie's eyes bore into me as if she knows something I don't. She almost certainly does.

I am repeatedly tempted to open my eyes to see is she still there, but I resist. When I finish meditating and open my eyes, she is gone.

–

Monday 9 January

Buddha: 'Meditate ... do not delay, lest you later regret it.' Right, then.

–

Tuesday 10 January

Buddhist tradition says that while meditation is necessary for spiritual progress, it is not sufficient. One needs to make broader changes to one's life in order to carry the benefits of meditation into all areas: work, home life, friends. The purpose of meditation is not to have a perfect meditation sit (thank goodness!), but to transform one's life more broadly: to see things as they really are, cultivate compassion and attain greater calmness throughout all parts of the day.

'Calmness throughout all parts of the day' certainly eludes me today. Today is a helter-skelter whirlwind of consultations, meetings, phone calls, emails and heaven knows what else. I struggle to remain in control of the flow of information and events. At some point I lose track of what I'm doing and what I'm supposed to be doing and simply keep on blindly *doing*. Eventually, I work my way through the dense thicket of activities and reach a clearing or, rather, a spot in the undergrowth where I can see and list everything that needs to be done before going home. I then move along more purposefully.

I appear weirdly calm through all of this, but I need to work more on my inner calm. Hopefully, meditation will help.

–

Wednesday 11 January

Okay. This might sound obvious, but meditation works much better when I have fewer distractions, for example, at home before everyone is up or in the office before 9 am and after 5 pm. Lunchtime is bad because I'm in the middle of a working day and it's more difficult to detach – but perhaps that means I should deliberately try to meditate then because it's when I need it most? For now, still in the opening stages of my project, I think I'd better stick with times when it's easier to focus: I need some easy wins until I get settled into the thing. Fifteen minutes fly past. Still distracted but doing okay. Good enough is good enough.

–

Thursday 12 January

Zen saying: 'Where there is great doubt, there will be great awakening; small doubt, small awakening; no doubt, no awakening.' This is reassuring. I have great, great doubt.

–

Friday 13 January

George, a man in his twenties, comes to see me in the psychiatry clinic today. George has lost interest in his business studies, distanced himself from friends and family and has no enthusiasm for his usual activities. On further questioning it turns out he has also lost weight, cannot sleep much of the time and feels futile almost all of the time. George asks if he is depressed or if this is just part of the normal ups and downs of life.

I have never been depressed in the way George is, so when he asks if I really understand how he feels, I am honest and say, No, I don't fully understand because I've never felt the way he feels. Over the years I've seen thousands of people who have felt this way and asked each of them, like I ask George, to explain exactly how they feel, so that I can understand better. I just sit quietly and listen to George as he speaks at length.

Another Zen saying: 'Sitting quietly doing nothing, spring comes, grass grows of itself.'

I meditate after work. I leave my patients behind me when I go home. This is a necessary habit rather than a choice. I will often work on a research project or write an article at home, especially in the early morning, but clinical work always stays in the workplace. So when I settle down to meditate, George's story and those of all my other patients have been left behind and all I have are my own feelings after the day: satisfaction (sometimes), frustration (more commonly than I would like) and, inevitably, tiredness. Is tiredness a 'feeling'? I certainly feel it. In fact, I feel it right now. Enough!

–

Saturday 14 January

The weekend! Up early for a couple of hours' work and fifteen minutes of moderate meditation before everyone else wakes up. Splendid. It's very, very annoying, I know, but I *love* mornings.

I spend much of the day with my family but in the afternoon I go to the Irish Film Institute to see a new film, *The Wonder Eye*, about the psychiatrist Ivor Browne. Part of the First Fortnight mental health arts festival in the IFI, the movie is subtitled *Meetings with Ivor* and includes footage of a number of people having conversations with Browne, a prominent psychiatrist and reformer of Ireland's mental health service. The movie is fascinating, apart from the bits with me in them, which make me cringe.

Sunday 15 January

Up early. I work for a couple of hours and meditate for fifteen minutes. Afterwards I have green tea, which always tastes better after meditation. The Tao of tea.

While I might not be a good – or even vaguely adequate – meditator yet, this process has already made me more aware of my mind and how distracted I become. This is most obvious in the contrast between morning and evening: in the morning, my mind is sharper and more focused; in the evening, it is a hopeless mess of distraction and chaos.

–

Monday 16 January

I do an interview with, of all people, Swiss National Radio. They spotted a short piece I wrote in *The Lancet* over Christmas about medical romance novels – dashing doctors, dedicated nurses, critically ill patients (who miraculously survive) and babies who pop up from nowhere providing the inevitable happy ending. In 2007 I wrote a light-hearted piece in *The Lancet* after reading twenty such novels and followed it up ten years later by reading twenty more. I've no idea why. This time round I found that little changes in the world of medical romance: hearts melt, wounds heal and love triumphs every time, especially in the emergency room and in airborne medical teams.

I have a good chat with Swiss National Radio who ask if medical romance novels reflect reality (no), if I know why these novels are so popular (life! death! romance! what's not to like?) and if the radio station can call me again in ten years' time to see if I've read twenty more medical romance novels. I say yes, they can call again: as long as *The Lancet* keep publishing, I'll keep reading.

I meditate for fifteen minutes, banishing all thought of medical romance from my mind.

Tuesday 17 January

What is happening in my head? Whenever I try to meditate, hundreds of thoughts rush in, thoughts about work, things I need to do, things I don't need to do, odd memories, random musings, thoughts about thoughts, thoughts about thoughts about thoughts and so on. It's difficult to stop *forcing* these thoughts away and *forcing* my focus back to my breath. This forcing is a problem because it is too active, too aggressive, too futile. It magnifies the distraction. Instead, I need to let the intrusive thoughts drift past without engaging with them.

This is difficult. Usually, I engage with the thoughts by either thinking about them or trying to force them away. Both options represent engagement and distraction, and both are to be avoided.

Most frustrating of all, I often think about how I need to let intruding thoughts drift past but fail to do so, and this thought itself becomes a further form of engagement and distraction. I need to stop *thinking* about letting the intrusive thoughts drift past (and how I fail to do so) and simply *let* them drift past instead.

In other words, don't just think it, do it. Let it happen.

–

Wednesday 18 January

I have a long-standing interest in Buddhism. In 2010 I completed a superb distance-learning course in Buddhist studies at the University of Sunderland with plenty of online discussion, group activities, seminars and assignments. I learned lots. Looking back, I can't help wondering if I did the course with the subconscious intention of avoiding meditating, just like I buy books about mindfulness as if that is just as useful as actually practising mindfulness. (It isn't.) Perhaps these are all just ways of avoiding the commitment to and necessary discipline of meditation – by distracting myself with books and articles and thoughts and thoughts about thoughts and heaven knows what else.

All is quiet as I sit, apart from the wind outside the window and the tram passing every few minutes, bringing people home. Soon, I too go home.

Thursday 19 January

So far, I've been doing (or trying to do) a meditation practice known as the 'mindfulness of breathing'. A mindfulness exercise such as this is a good way to start or restart meditation because it focuses on, well, focus. Specifically, it helps to establish and polish up the skills involved in concentrating the mind on the present moment.

Today, however, just to shake it up a little, I try a 'loving kindness' meditation that I learned many years ago, whereby I spend a few minutes trying to feel loving kindness for myself, then for someone for whom it is easy to feel loving kindness (a family member or friend), then for someone neutral (a random person I saw in a shop earlier), and then for someone for whom I find it difficult to feel loving kindness (no shortage of candidates there, sadly). I finish by trying to feel loving kindness for the whole world and all living beings in it – a tall order.

That, in any case, is the theory. In practice, I spend most of today's fifteen minutes yawning and forgetting for whom I'm supposed to be feeling loving kindness. Loving kindness is not easy to summon up at will, but that's the whole point: this practice is supposed to make loving kindness into a habit. It's clearly still far from being a habit for me.

Still, this meditation practice puts the idea of loving kindness firmly back into my head and maybe if I practise more I'll get the hang of it. But not today.

–

Friday 20 January

Twenty days in and – first things first – I'm happy and surprised that I'm still meditating each day. It is always imperfect but I always do it. Today was especially difficult. I was on *The Tommy Tiernan Show* on RTÉ television last night talking about mental health and suicide. It's an entirely unscripted show. Mr Tiernan has no idea who the guests are until they walk onto the stage so there is absolutely no preparation. It is all spontaneous and my interview was wide-ranging and very open. As a result, my work today is punctuated by messages, emails and phone calls with responses to the show, follow-up queries and requests for second opinions.

In the afternoon I see George again. He is still feeling depressed but, he says, is not without hope. We talk at some length and agree that he will see a psychotherapist on a weekly basis in order to discuss how he feels, explore his habitual thinking and behaviour patterns and figure out ways to amend these to improve his mood. He asks about medication and I say it would be reasonable to try an antidepressant if he wants to but also quite reasonable just to try psychotherapy on its own. George opts for psychotherapy alone and I advise him to stop drinking alcohol: the more you drink, the more likely you are to be depressed. We will meet again in a month to see how he's getting on.

I cycle home in reflective mood. Later, as I try to meditate, I keep thinking not about George but, oddly, about why I'm *not* thinking about my patients after such an intense day. I sometimes identify quite strongly with my patients and sometimes not at all. Starting out in psychiatry, it's hard not to compare yourself to your patients, wondering if their symptoms could enter your life. But this tendency diminishes over time. It's not that one becomes more distant but rather that one stops comparing oneself with others so minutely. I try to just sit for fifteen minutes without comparing myself to anybody, with moderate success. I will try again tomorrow.

–

Saturday 21 January
Buddha: 'Ardently do today what must be done. Who knows? Tomorrow, death comes.' That's a bit dark, surely? I sit for fifteen uninterrupted minutes and there is a mild calming effect that is pleasant if short-lived.

–

Sunday 22 January
The birds outside the window are in full voice. It's a radiant morning: cool, crisp and perfect for walking to the cinema, which I duly do. I love the cinema and can spend endless hours there, lost to the world. Immersion in the cinema is calming and settling. It is not quite a form of meditation but it is an escape from moment-to-moment reality and

from the deadening drumbeat of conscious thought. Now that I think about it, is going to the cinema the opposite of meditation? An explicit retreat from the reality of the present moment into unreality? Either way, I love it. Perhaps both pursuits are needed.

–

Monday 23 January
Each month, as well as reflecting on a specific theme (this month, the first noble truth of Buddhism, *duhkha*, the kind of unsatisfactoriness I experienced *even in Paris*), I am also reading a book from the enormous stack of mindfulness guides and Buddhist books I have accumulated over the years. Buying so many books is undoubtedly a way of avoiding the discipline of meditation. I have read some but not all of them. If I read them all, I would have no time to meditate or, indeed, do anything else.

This month I reread parts of *One City: A Declaration of Interdependence* by Ethan Nichtern, an excellent book about living a life informed by Buddhist values in modern, urban settings. It explores the fundamental inter-connectedness of everything in the world – the *real* internet, which manages to be both analogous with and somehow opposite to the computer-based internet. Plenty of food for thought here, encouraging me to remember that the urban environment in which I live is a community of people and that everyone and everything is profoundly interdependent.

–

Tuesday 24 January
Lots of unsatisfactoriness today. I meditate for fifteen reasonable minutes before work, focusing on my breathing. Presumably so many meditation practices focus on the breath in order to prevent you thinking about other things. Focusing on the breath also makes the meditation practice universal and portable: everyone has breath to focus on. Those who do not have breath to focus on have much greater problems. I am lucky to be breathing today. Here's hoping for tomorrow.

Wednesday 25 January

Still breathing today! It's 6 am and I sit trying to meditate for fifteen minutes. Very distracted today: it's chilly, the birds are singing outside the window and I need tea. I have a mild addiction to green tea. Presumably, it's okay for me to be mindful of all these things because they belong in the present moment but I am also distracted by them and have difficulty returning focus to my breath.

For some reason, today's meditation reminds me strongly of the mindfulness courses I attended in the distant past, and how frustrating I found them. This was attributable to my own distraction and lack of commitment, rather than the teachers, who were mostly excellent. In addition, many people at these courses seemed to skip over the hard bits, the actual mindfulness. Some people seemed oddly blissed out anyway, regardless of what happened; some were obsessed with technical details that seemed very minor to me; and others were sending surreptitious text messages on their phones.

There seems to be a thin line between mindfulness and mindlessness. Or, at the very least, mindfulness and mindlessness are not quite the opposites they initially sound like. I can't decide if the birds outside the window are mindful, mindless, or neither. Maybe they've transcended mind?

At work I see three homeless patients one after the other. They are all depressed. But do their circumstances explain their depression? Is it reasonable to describe someone as 'depressed' when their mental state is at least partially understandable in the context of their life circumstances? Either way, regardless of whether one says these three individuals are 'depressed' or not, it is clear that they are suffering deeply and most of the solutions lie in improving their social and personal circumstances. That is what we focus on today.

But days like today can be depressing for me. I feel powerless. Hopefully, meditation will help me better manage feelings like this. Today, I simply plough on.

Thursday 26 January

I'm getting better at meditating before work. I'm still distracted but I'm definitely improving. For the first time, I am disappointed when my phone makes the wind chimes noise to indicate fifteen minutes have passed.

This is good news in as far as it goes but I know that I need to extend a sense of mindfulness more generally into my day, outside of my meditation sits. For example, I'm typing these words into this journal at the same time as I'm eating a sandwich for lunch and keeping an eye on my emails. I think this multitasking is inconsistent with what is known as 'mindful eating'. When you type, just type. When you eat, just eat. So, I'll stop typing now and do just that.

–

Friday 27 January

My thoughts wander, for no apparent reason, to April 2011 when the Dalai Lama, world-renowned Tibetan Buddhist monk and teacher, visited Ireland. To mark the occasion I took some leave and hit the road for two days to hear him speak at Citywest Hotel in Dublin on the morning of 13 April, St Brigid's Cathedral, Kildare, that afternoon and the University of Limerick the following morning. The Dalai Lama was a smiling, happy figure, stopping in the crowds to shake hands and pausing to greet people.

The Dalai Lama's appearance in St Brigid's Cathedral in Kildare was especially affecting and my rather gentle two-day Dalai Lama road trip was simply lovely: quiet, solitary, peaceful. The offbeat highlight was, perhaps, seeing monks in saffron robes chatting and laughing in a hotel bar on the outskirts of Limerick as I ate my decidedly non-Buddhist burger. I must try to see the Dalai Lama again at some point.

But for now, I wonder, will meditating affect how I work, how I relate to patients and how I relate to families of patients? We will see. Or will we? How will I know if anything changes? Will I notice? Will anyone tell me?

Saturday 28 January

Buddha: 'The one in whom no longer exist the craving and thirst that perpetuate becoming; how could you track that Awakened one, trackless, and of limitless range?'

–

Sunday 29 January

I start the day with a body scan. This is a mindfulness technique aimed at becoming more aware of yourself, rooted in the body's position and sensations at the present moment. I start with awareness of my breathing, shift my focus to my feet and then slowly move my focus up through my body until I reach the tip of my head. It's a lovely exercise. Although my thoughts wander intermittently, I bring them back gently each time.

The fifteen-minute meditation sit goes better today, possibly because I am up and full of beans at 6 am. Afterwards I work for a few hours in the quiet of the early morning, birds ever present outside the window and Trixie gazing at me silently. That cat seems 100 per cent mindful all of the time, as well as 100 per cent ready to enjoy cheese at any moment in a charming, unselfconscious way.

I understand that I should not give her cheese.

But I do.

–

Monday 30 January

I commonly experience what I will call 'post-meditation irritability' whereby (a) the world seems intolerably noisy and annoying for five or ten minutes after meditation, (b) I am irritated that I failed to meditate better and (c) the annoyance and irritation vanish after twenty minutes or so and everything carries on as normal. I trust this will diminish as time goes by.

Tuesday 31 January

It takes at least three months to establish a new habit. This month has been all about starting a modest, sustainable meditation habit in contrast to my previous efforts, which were uneven, overambitious and fairly random. With this in mind I've spent ten or fifteen minutes trying to meditate each day for the past month. I have not missed any days. What have I learned so far?

- Meditation is challenging.
- Everything is better in the morning.
- I meditate best sitting firmly upright in a chair with my arms on the arm rests or on my knees.
- For fifteen minutes of meditation it is best to settle down and then set the timer on the phone for *sixteen* minutes so that I feel relaxed about starting to focus and not under pressure because the clock has started ticking.
- As soon as I try to clear my mind, thoughts come crowding into my head at an astonishing rate. These thoughts are very varied and include the predictable, the unpredictable, the random and the profoundly bizarre. It is especially difficult when I think of something that is genuinely important as I try to clear my mind. I still need to let that thought pass without engaging with it, no matter how important it seems at the time. This is difficult. I've possibly become marginally better at it over the past month, but only very marginally.
- Finally, I have learned that there is no definite benefit from spending ten or fifteen minutes trying to meditate each day for a month. The only demonstrable positive so far is that I have actually done it. That does give me a certain satisfaction. I appear to have attained administrative consistency rather than spiritual enlightenment. Perhaps that is enough for now.

That's it. In many ways, this is exactly what I expected. I'm at the start of a year-long project and there are eleven more months to go. One must be realistic. For the next month I need to commit more firmly to a full fifteen minutes of daily meditation and continue to improve my focus.

I eat some cake to mark the end of the first month in my meditation project. It is a slice of almost-forgotten chocolate cake, lurking in a container all on its own at the back of the press, like a piece of driftwood stranded on the beach after the tide has gone out. How did everyone else forget about it?

It is delicious.

February

—

In which I try to consolidate my modest meditation habit and extend the effects of meditation into other areas of my life. By and large, I fail. I continue to feel disproportionately irritated at minor upsets and to experience anger for reasons that are either very minor or very vague or both. I eat meat despite knowing that I should respect all sentient beings. On the plus side, I continue stubbornly to meditate daily for fifteen minutes although I cannot decide if I am doing so owing to a self-defeating 'craving' for progress, old-fashioned pig-headedness or simply in order to avoid more challenging pursuits such as going running. Still, I carry on meditating even if the reasons are becoming more and more obscure.

Wednesday 1 February

I start a new month by meditating for fifteen minutes at lunchtime. I also start the month by going to the cinema in the evening and eating a burger afterwards – a most un-Buddhist activity (the burger, not the movie). In Hinduism, cows are considered sacred and treated with great respect. Buddhism, in contrast, does not single out particular living creatures for specific mention but says that all life is sacred and should be profoundly respected. Human life is especially valuable because it offers unique opportunity for spiritual advancement but, in Buddhism, any living creature can be reincarnated as a human, or might have been human in a previous life, so all life must be respected. And that includes cows.

–

Thursday 2 February

Last month's theme in my meditation project was *duhkha*, the first noble truth of Buddhism, which refers to the unsatisfactoriness of human experience. This month's theme is the second noble truth, which is the cause of *duhkha*. In Buddhist tradition *duhkha* is caused by craving, hatred and delusion. These experiences are most often implicit in our responses to sensory phenomena. This truth provides much of the basis for Buddhism's focus on cognition, cognitive training and the practice of meditation.

And today it goes okay. It is important not to crave too much for better meditation skills. Too much craving only leads to *duhkha*.

–

Friday 3 February

Zen saying: 'If you understand, things are just as they are; if you do not understand, things are just as they are.' So perhaps none of my agonising matters. Perhaps nobody's agonising matters. Perhaps, but that is not the whole story: the suffering involved in agonising matters greatly.

At work I see a woman with panic attacks. Around once a week, when Maura is in a public place like a supermarket, she develops acute anxiety, feels her heart racing and thinks she is about to die. The logical part of Maura's brain knows she is not going to die but the logical part of her brain is overwhelmed by the rush of rising anxiety. She feels she has to leave the situation. She abandons her shopping trolley and rushes to her car. She feels safe there. Maura's anxiety subsides after a while but she is shaken by the experience for the rest of the day. What disturbs her most is that she knows her anxiety is irrational and excessive and yet it recurs. Why?

Listening to Maura today, I'm struck by two things. Firstly, how familiar Maura's story is: I've seen hundreds, even thousands of people with this complaint over the years. But this story is not familiar to Maura: it's all new and scary for her and she needs help.

Secondly, I'm struck by the centrality of compassion in this situation. I know that we can help Maura with information, reassurance, psychological therapy and possibly other forms of treatment and support if needed. But compassion comes first and this is something that I've noticed over the past few weeks as I've tried to meditate more often. I don't think I have any more compassion than I had before I started meditating daily but I have certainly come to appreciate its significance. This might or might not be a lasting effect. We will see.

–

Saturday 4 February

Lovely morning, a welcome break from the rain of the past two days. I get up at 6 am, work for an hour, meditate for fifteen minutes and work for a further hour. The rest of the day involves various family activities and a great deal of driving around. Most importantly: it does not rain. I even make it to the cinema in the afternoon.

–

Sunday 5 February

I am on call today, which means I spend much of the day in the hospital, assessing people with mental health problems. I also take phone calls at home during the night and return to the hospital if needed. Being on call can be very intense, especially when a busy day at work is followed by a disturbed night, which is then followed by another busy day at work. And so, arriving home this evening around nine pm and facing into a night of phone calls from the hospital (and possibly another trip in), I manage a distracted fifteen minutes of meditation, with an ear out for the phone at all times. These are unsatisfactory conditions for meditation but one must take the rough with the smooth.

–

Monday 6 February

There was just one phone call from the hospital in the middle of the night last night, so while I'm certainly tired today, I have been a million times more tired on previous occasions when the nights have been much busier. Psychiatry is far from being a nine-to-five job: most mental health crises occur in the evenings and at weekends, and mental health services need to respond in the acute hospitals at all hours of the day and night. I am once again seized by the difficulties faced by people with mental illness and their families, especially the discrimination and social exclusion they so often experience. I write academic papers and books on this topic but twenty-four hours on call never fails to make these problems very real and raw to me again.

Against this background I think it is important to occasionally move outside the academic field and write about these themes in the general media. From a young age I have written letters to the editors of newspapers and magazines, often concerning systematic discrimination against the mentally ill and their increased rates of homelessness and imprisonment.

Writing letters to be published in newspapers is a peculiar pursuit. Oscar Wilde had his doubts about the entire enterprise: 'I am afraid that writing to newspapers has a deteriorating influence on style. People get violent, and abusive, and lose all sense of proportion, when they enter that curious journalistic arena in which the race is always to the noisiest.' P.G. Wodehouse had a different view: 'I yearn to write letters to the papers. All authors do. Novelists are merely those who have failed as contributors to the Correspondence Column. Unable to make the grade, they drop down a rung on the ladder and write novels.'

I'm with P.G. Wodehouse. It's worth taking every opportunity to comment publicly about improving mental health and social services and increasing public understanding of mental illness. No matter how minor the contribution seems, it will reach somebody, somewhere, sometime. It all adds up in quiet, inevitable ways, like snow falling gently in the darkness across an uneven, unknowable landscape.

–

Tuesday 7 February

I am fond of statues of Buddha and have dozens of them all over the house. My favourite is a bronze in the lotus position with dark red and turquoise inlay that I bought in a market in Bangalore last year. I almost exceeded my baggage capacity on the flight home but my Indian Buddha now has pride of place in the kitchen.

I am also very fond of a large, almost life-size, outdoor Buddha in the back garden, made of dark, hard plastic. My garden Buddha is seated with legs folded in the lotus position, meditating. The statue's origins are not especially spiritual. I bought it in a suburban garden centre on a Saturday afternoon a few years ago. The statue would not fit in the boot of the car so I sat it on the passenger seat and put the seat belt around it. Because it is almost life-size, it looked like I had a meditating Buddha sitting beside me in the car, much to the astonishment of the driver next to me at the traffic lights.

Unlike my garden Buddha I find the lotus position impossible to assume. Most cross-legged meditation positions just too painful for me. So today, as usual, I sit in a chair. I'm not as calm as Buddha but I think I'm calmer than I used to be. Or perhaps I'm just imagining it. I wonder is there a meaningful difference between those two possibilities, how calm I am and how calm I think I am? Are they the same thing?

Wednesday 8 February

Buddha: 'Give, even if you only have a little.' The widow's mite?

–

Thursday 9 February

I'm pretty exhausted today after a night on call but I plough through work in the morning and attend meetings in town in the afternoon. By six pm it is urgently necessary to go to the cinema in order to rebalance, so I see *Denial* in the IFI, a good movie about Holocaust denial. Later I have trouble dispelling the snowy images of Auschwitz from my mind. I visited Auschwitz ten years ago and found it very affecting. Once I get home I try to dispel the images and focus on my breath. I do not succeed.

–

Friday 10 February

Finally the week draws to a close. It's a distracted, peculiar day at work filled with administration and, thankfully, time with junior doctors doing research projects under my supervision. I also see Maura again. Her panic attacks are persisting and she requests antidepressant medication in addition to the psychological therapy I recommended last week. We have a discussion and she decides to try the medication in conjunction with psychological therapy: 'I'll try anything,' she says, utterly exhausted by her anxiety. We have a good discussion, we make a new plan and off she goes.

The day is all fairly satisfying in the end, if a little tiring. I tidy up after the week: answer outstanding emails, file away endless papers and drafts of projects and make phone calls. At home, I eat, read newspapers, meditate with moderate focus and write in this journal. The cat, Trixie, is in contemplative, end-of-week mood too. She sits with that deep, deep stillness I envy so much, gazing imperturbably ahead with occasional, solemn, unhurried blinks. Bed.

Saturday 11 February

I'm working to a deadline to finish a book, *Mental Health in Ireland*. It is a guide to mental health and common mental illnesses aimed at the general public and interested professionals. Writing it has been a protracted process but I'm in the final stretches now. I hope the book proves helpful for people in distress, people encountering mental illness for the first time and families struggling with unfamiliar concepts. As well as common mental illnesses, I deal in the book with some especially challenging topics: involuntary admission to psychiatric hospitals, deliberate self-harm, suicide and murder-suicide. I also include chapters on mental wellness, happiness, dignity and, of course, mindfulness. I need more of that myself!

–

Sunday 12 February

I have had an interest in meditation and mental health for well over a decade, linking my personal interest in contemplative practice with my professional life. I write about this a little more in 'Meditation, Mindfulness and Mental Health' (p. 61). Reflecting on this theme, I am struck by the fact that it is 'mindfulness' rather than 'meditation' that has become a buzzword over the intervening decade. I worry occasionally that something important is lost when mindfulness, although very useful, becomes somewhat unmoored from meditation, which invariably lies at the heart of true contemplative practice.

–

Monday 13 February

The birds are singing as I meditate early this morning. Also, a house alarm is making a beeping sound. The alarm is not going off loudly. It is just making an intermittent, persistent, dysfunctional-sounding beep. It bothers me but does not seem to bother the birds, who continue singing regardless.

Or do they?

As I fail to meditate I wonder how we know that the birds are actually singing. Perhaps they're chatting. Or maybe their 'song' is the sound that birds make when they're in pain. Maybe the birdsong that sounds so sweet to us is the avian equivalent of howls of agony. How would we know? Good grief, I need to get a grip. I have a cup of green tea to settle myself.

–

Tuesday 14 February
Valentine's day – a day of romance. I give a lecture about erotomania in Trinity College as part of a series of seminars on the medical humanities. The full title is 'Love as Delusion, Delusions of Love: Erotomania and the Modern Mind'.

Erotomania is a rare psychiatric condition in which the patient ('subject') develops the delusion (fixed, false belief) that he or she is loved from afar by another person ('object'). The subject is generally female, though males predominate in prisons and secure hospitals. The object is generally perceived to belong to a higher social class, often seems unattainable (for example a celebrity) and is usually believed to be the first to declare love. The onset of the delusion is classically sudden but may be gradual. The subject will often cite far-fetched 'proof' of the object's affections and may paradoxically interpret rejections as covert declarations of love. It is a rare, interesting disorder.

Today's talk focuses on delusions of love – whether if it is possible to have a delusion that one is in love and not really be in love. I have no idea if this is possible and even if it were, Valentine's Day is hardly the day to suggest that loving relationships might be based on delusions! Nonetheless, that is exactly what I do. I have no idea why. The talk and discussion are good fun.

In the evening I place all thoughts of romance aside and meditate for fifteen minutes.

Wednesday 15 February

There is an infinite number of quotes from Buddha on the internet. I wonder how many are genuine or, at least, how many find roots, however distant, in Buddhist scripture. Here is one: 'One is not called noble who harms living beings. By not harming living beings one is called noble.' That's all very well, but did Buddha really say it? Or does it matter if he said it or not?

—

Thursday 16 February

I struggle to find the energy to keep going. More Buddha: 'Speak only endearing speech, speech that is welcomed. Speech, when it brings no evil to others, is a pleasant thing.' I try to speak well to everyone I meet during the day, but I've no way of knowing how I'm doing. Perhaps I'll never know.

—

Friday 17 February

Friday. An oddly settling day at work as various loose ends obediently allow themselves to be tied up. A bit like Trixie when she refrains from mischief around the house: you can't predict when it will happen and when it does you just go with it.

In the evening we head off for a family weekend in Sligo where I'm giving a talk at a meeting of GPs about the Assisted Decision-Making (Capacity) Act 2015. This an interesting, ambitious piece of legislation seeking to better protect the autonomy of people with impaired mental capacity. I'm involved in implementation so I try to speak about it whenever I'm invited to educational meetings.

I sandwich in a brief meditation somewhere in the day. I forget where, precisely.

Saturday 18 February

After an appalling night's sleep in the hotel in Sligo I end up sitting in the car in the hotel car park at 5 am, working on my computer and then meditating. If anyone comes along and sees me they'll think I'm asleep or drunk or dead. Meditation is, in many ways, the opposite of drinking alcohol. Meditation involves focusing fully on the present moment and seeing things as they really are, without any distortions and without clouding one's mind in any way.

I can, however, report that sitting in a car in a hotel car park in the chilly early morning in mid February is not especially conducive to meditation. Still, I do my best and then go for a walk around Sligo town: quiet streets, deserted squares, shops with their shutters down. The town's silence is oddly meditative and the walk brings me closer to clarity and reality than the meditation does. The silence is especially moving. I recall reading about silence last month, but silence can really only be experienced. Reading about silence is like writing about music or dancing about architecture. You can certainly do it but it falls well short of the real thing.

–

Sunday 19 February

Yesterday we met with friends in Strandhill. We visit the Niland Collection in Sligo's Model arts centre and climb Knocknarea, a large hill west of Sligo town, to visit the tomb of Queen Medb. We last did this climb several years ago on a lovely, clear day with wild, wide views out to the Atlantic. We take a new path to the summit. A dense mist blows in from the sea. It is ridiculously atmospheric at the peak: Celtic, mystical and very, very damp. At another time of year this would be a lovely spot for meditation but today it is wet beyond description. One cannot meditate while sopping wet.

Monday 20 February

This month, instead of reading a book about meditation or Buddhist studies, I'm revisiting the November 2010 edition of *Contemporary Buddhism*, a special issue devoted to U Dhammaloka, 'the Irish Buddhist'. U Dhammaloka, whose original name is not certain, lived from approximately 1856 to 1914. He was an Irish-born migrant worker who was ordained as a Buddhist monk in Burma some time before 1900, making him one of the earliest attested western Buddhist monks. He was also an atheist critic of Christian missionaries and a temperance campaigner. He took an active role in the Asian Buddhist revival at that time and the papers in this special edition explore several aspects of his life and work. They are thoughtful and fascinating.

U Dhammaloka is a reminder that globalisation – although it has gathered pace in recent decades – is not entirely new. I meditate gently for a while but I also think about U Dhammaloka and his unusual, peripatetic life. I hope he was happy.

–

Tuesday 21 February

This month's theme in my meditation project is the second noble truth, the causes of *duhkha*, which are craving, hatred and delusion. Can one examine these things in oneself? I think I'm okay with respect to 'hatred' (I can't think of much that I hate although I suppose there are many things I dislike) but craving and delusion (clinging to false beliefs) present far greater challenges. It's hard not to want things and harder still not to cling to less-than-true ideas about oneself and the world.

Still, Buddhism suggests that learning to focus on the present moment helps such illusions simply to fall away. I try to do that today, with moderate effect.

Wednesday 22 February

One of the temptations experienced by people starting to meditate is that they head off on a retreat for a week or weekend and do some intense meditation but then fail to integrate meditation into their daily lives back home. I think I'm falling into the lesser described, opposite trap: *only* trying to meditate for small snippets of time during day-to-day life and *never* seeking a more sustained period of meditating outside the run of daily affairs. I will keep an eye out for opportunities to remedy this by going on a retreat or the like but for today I stick with my rather unglamorous fifteen minutes in my usual daily setting.

It's not exactly thrilling but I expect it's better than not meditating at all.

—

Thursday 23 February

I'm a little worried about Trixie. She looks quite anxious when I get home this evening but then she sleeps for many, many hours on the sofa before waking briefly, stretching and getting into her bed to sleep all night. I meditate for an unsatisfactory fifteen minutes before bed and then sleep poorly. I have much to learn from that cat.

—

Friday 24 February

This morning Trixie arrives home from her early-morning jaunt in a rough state. She's clearly been in a fight, probably with another cat who dared to enter our back garden, despite it being Trixie's territory. Trixie doesn't seem to be injured so presumably her opponent got the worst of the encounter. I'm just thankful she hasn't brought home a dead mouse or worse, a live one. Or worse again, a dead duckling. All have, sadly, featured in the past. Despite the daily prospect of such carnage, I meditate grimly on.

At work George returns to see me a month after I recommended psychotherapy for his depression. The clinic where I see him is a standard health-system facility, serviceable and durable. It's the people who make it work: the unfailingly helpful receptionist and administrative staff, the allied health professionals in various offices throughout the building, my psychiatrist colleagues and the team of junior doctors we supervise. All patients see a consultant psychiatrist at some point and follow-up care is dispersed across the disciplines and grades depending on evolving need. At the moment, I'm seeing George myself because he lives in the geographical catchment area covered by our team and I saw him the first time he presented to us. But we work as a team and George will inevitably see other team members at different times: nurses, psychologists, occupational therapists, social workers and many others.

George is much more positive. He sits calmly in the chair by the window of my consulting room. (Contrary to popular belief, we do not have couches.) George saw the psychotherapist I recommended last month but did not find it helpful. This is not uncommon: psychotherapy is quite a personalised undertaking and sometimes it just doesn't work out. He then saw a different psychotherapist for two sessions and established a much better relationship with her. She has agreed to see him weekly for ten weeks and then review progress. This is good. George knows what he wants and has somewhere found the energy and optimism to work towards recovery. He has also stopped drinking for now, which will also help.

All I can do today is endorse George's progress and suggest he makes some modest changes to his diet and establishes a sustainable exercise pattern. He looks at me witheringly as I spout advice and asks me if I exercise every day. He makes a good point. I shut up. I'll see him again in a couple of months, sooner if he wants.

I know he'll be fine. I tell him this.

–

Saturday 25 February
Thinking a lot about *duhkha* and its causes: craving, hatred and delusion. I wonder did U Dhammaloka conquer them? I have not. All are present today at least to a certain extent. I take a break from worrying about this in order to meditate. Perhaps that's the trick – ignore the

problems and perhaps they'll go away. This has been one of my tried-and-tested approaches to life's problems over the years and it works out well more often than one might expect. Fingers crossed this time.

–

Sunday 26 February

Instead of meditating indoors, I sit outside during one of the longer breaks between rain showers. I have a cup of tea and then casually start meditating. To all intents and purposes, passers-by will think I'm just sitting there but I am, in fact, focusing on my breathing. A few neighbours greet me and I respond briefly then settle back into meditating with unexpected ease. It all feels easier outside. There are more external distractions but fewer internal ones. This is not at all how I thought it would be. It is a good step forward.

–

Monday 27 February

Back to work. I meditate in the early morning and then do a day's work. It's a busy one because today is the publisher's deadline for my new book. I meet the deadline with around ten minutes to spare. What's the panic?

At home Trixie is extra affectionate for some reason. There are no visible signs of a fight and, thankfully, no corpses of small animals either. Killing is very un-Buddhist and I like to think that Trixie is an elevated, meditative cat rather than a cold-blooded killer. That, perhaps, is another of my delusions as I crave the belief that my cat is an enlightened being. I dislike the fact that clearly she is not.

There's your *duhkha* right there: delusion and unsatisfactoriness all around.

And that's just the cat.

Tuesday 28 February

Maura returns. She is feeling significantly but not completely better. She's having fewer panic attacks and feels she can soon return to work. Her husband agrees she's much improved. I'm delighted. I presume it's OK to feel a sense of satisfaction at this? Maura has made an excellent start towards recovery and has a good understanding of what she needs to do from this point onwards.

Obviously it's Maura who is putting in the real work here, not me – I'm just doing my job. But the nature of my work makes it feel like so much more than just a job: it is so human, so intense, so personal. Of course one needs to strike a balance between connection with the patient on the one hand and professional distance on the other, but, oddly, this is not as difficult as it sounds: one can be professional and also engaged with the person in front of you. Both are achievable and both are essential. No one wants mental health care from a vending machine.

And as for me, I can't believe a second month has passed in my twelve-month meditation project. To mark the occasion, I eat cake. This month I have two small buns with bright pink icing that I bought at a school cake sale last Sunday. The cake-to-icing ratio is superb, so the month ends with me essentially getting high on sugar. I'm not certain Buddha would approve.

March

—

In which spring finally arrives, I continue to meditate and it remains impossible to judge whether or not I'm making progress. On the plus side Trixie is much more settled. She, at least, appears to benefit from my meditation project. Perhaps that is enough? That would be true altruism: if the cat benefits and I do not, I should simply be happy for the cat. Buddhism teaches that we are each continuous with the broader world: the suffering of others is my suffering too; the happiness of others is my happiness too. But I dearly wish that my newly happy cat would stop killing other creatures and dragging home their bloodied corpses. It is most un-Buddhist of her. Clearly there is still work to be done for her to achieve full enlightenment. I must also meditate more. And better. This month, I try very hard. And, in an unusual turn of events, I join a gym. It's gym life, but not as we know it.

Wednesday 1 March

It is an inauspicious start to the month: dark, wet and dreary. Nonetheless, I meditate for fifteen minutes in the morning and proceed through the day: meetings, assessing patients, catching up on various administrative matters. After work, and an un-Buddhist burger, I make it to a movie, *Moonlight*, which has just won the 2017 Academy Award for Best Picture. It focuses on three stages in the life of a man as he gradually comes to terms with his sexuality. There's also plenty about the human cost of addiction and people's ambivalent attitudes to drugs. It's a thoughtful movie, very sad in its themes, but it's also a wonderful example of the power of cinema, which rarely fails to move me.

–

Thursday 2 March

Spring has come. I am 100 per cent certain of this. I have no solid basis for this belief apart from the sun being out but I'm going with it for now. I meditate jauntily (if such a thing is possible) in a spirit of optimism: drier, brighter days ahead! And a cup of green tea.

–

Friday 3 March

Buddha: 'Let all-embracing thoughts for all beings be yours.' Easier said than done.

–

Saturday 4 March

This month's theme in my year-long meditation project is the cessation of suffering. This is the idea that by facing *duhkha* (unsatisfactoriness) and overcoming craving, aversion and delusion, we can end suffering. This, the ultimate aim of Buddhist practice, is known as *nirvana* or *nibbana*. And this 'noble truth' also provides reason for hope: despite its ubiquity, suffering or unsatisfactoriness can be overcome.

The potential cessation of suffering is excellent news because I'm still on call and spend most of the day in the hospital dealing with mental health emergencies. It is interesting work but it takes a toll. Fifteen minutes of meditation is probably a good way to start a day like this one but the quality of my meditation is poor. I think this means I need it more than usual.

When I'm on call during the week I work as normal during the day and am mostly at home in the evenings and at night-time with my phone switched on. At weekends I'm in the hospital during the day and my phone remains on in the evenings and throughout the nights of Friday, Saturday and Sunday. Being available from 9 am on Friday until 5 pm or later on Monday is wearing, especially if I'm in the hospital at 2 am on one or more of the weekend nights. I don't always have to go into the hospital on those nights: I sometimes just deal with phone calls at home, lying in bed gazing nervously at my phone and waiting for it to ring again, failing miserably to sleep. This is the kind of anxiety that meditation should, perhaps, help with – but no sign of any progress yet.

–

Sunday 5 March
I am no longer on call. It would be an overstatement to describe simply not being on call as nirvana, but it's a definite improvement on the past two days. I meditate in the early morning, work on some research papers for an hour or so and spend the rest of the day walking on a windy Dún Laoghaire pier, hanging out and having pizza. I have always found Dún Laoghaire to be a strangely settling spot. The windswept west pier is my pier of choice. If you clamber over the wall away from the overgrown path there is solitude to be found – and waves and birds and the occasional seal. I like it here.

–

Monday 6 March
I am absolutely certain that spring has come. It is a lovely bright morning and I cycle to work for the first time in months. It is not an especially scenic ride, as my route is urban and suburban and even involves some motorway: there are off-road bicycle lanes for this part of the journey

and these are very relaxing, several metres removed from the thundering traffic. Spring, I conclude, has definitely, definitely, definitely arrived. There are even rabbits in Tymon Park. I stop and take a look. They do not scamper off. They just look at me, sniffing, wondering why I'm waving and chatting at them.

–

Tuesday 7 March

Today is a little less springy but the morning is dry and not unpleasant, so I meditate early in the spirit of spring. I really need to work hard to make this meditation meaningful and not just a tick-box exercise. I'm taking some days off work next week so perhaps I'll see about going to a formal meditation session, just to shake it up a little.

–

Wednesday 8 March

I meditate for fifteen minutes, do my day's work and then go to the Gate Theatre. The Gate is presenting a season of plays by three of the most iconic writers in modern theatre: Samuel Beckett, Brian Friel and Harold Pinter. This is the first of three evenings I will attend in this season of plays and today I see two short productions, *First Love* by Samuel Beckett and *The Dumb Waiter* by Harold Pinter. Between the two I pop out for noodles on Parnell Street.

I previously saw this production of *First Love*, featuring Barry McGovern, last October in the O'Reilly Theatre in nearby Belvedere College as part of the Dublin Theatre Festival. I have always loved Beckett and I'm currently reading his trilogy of novels, *Molloy*, *Malone Dies* and *The Unnamable*. I read two pages every night before bed. Never one page, never three pages, always two pages. It's a peculiar way of reading anything, I know, but it produces a steady rhythm and a useful pre-sleep ritual. I read *Ulysses* in this way some years ago. This system also allows me to read other books in parallel, while still keeping the reassuring rhythm of two pages per night humming along in the background. Odd as two left feet, I know, but I like it.

Thursday 9 March

In the middle of today's meditation, when I should be focusing on my breath, I have a realisation of sorts: since I started meditating, I notice my state of mind far more often than before. I commonly feel vaguely but significantly annoyed during the day. Around 10 per cent of the time, I find that my annoyance is entirely disproportionate to whatever caused it. And the other 90 per cent of the time *my annoyance has no cause whatsoever.*

It seems that I spend large chunks of time being annoyed at literally *nothing.* Over the years, I've probably spent months in this pointless, unsatisfactory state. Correcting it simply requires taking a few seconds to think about what has annoyed me before I realise that, most of the time, my annoyance has no cause. And then it vanishes.

This is, quite honestly, the first evidence of any kind of benefit from this meditation project: I've become a little more reflective about my moment-to-moment emotions and this has increased my clarity and decreased the amount of time I spend drifting about in a vaguely irritated, unfocused state. This is good.

–

Friday 10 March

I meditate poorly, preoccupied about a talk I'm giving in the afternoon. The dotMD meeting at Smock Alley Theatre in Dublin aims to expose healthcare professionals to ideas that take place at the interface of medicine, technology and the humanities. The intention is to inspire and reinvigorate these professionals and reawaken in them a sense of fun and curiosity about medicine. I very much enjoyed the meeting last year. This year's line-up includes doctors, scientists, innovators, writers, broadcasters, artists and a musician. My talk goes fine.

And I've certainly plenty to think about today. Earlier I saw Peter, a 21-year-old man with schizophrenia. Around a year ago, Peter – who had been perfectly well up until that point – began to distance himself from his family and friends. His college grades slipped and he took to staying at home all the time. Six months ago, he suddenly presented to the hospital's emergency department in a highly distressed state, saying he needed to be 'kept safe'. On further discussion, he said that certain websites had started to send him messages and while he did not actually hear voices, he described 'a feeling of voices' coming from outside his head. Websites, he said, were now controlling his thoughts. He was desperately unhappy.

Since that crisis presentation, Peter has been treated with antipsychotic medication and regular support from a community mental health nurse. Today, it is possible to treat someone like Peter at home, without necessarily admitting him to an inpatient psychiatric unit or hospital – and this is generally good. But I sometimes wonder if we have overshot the mark with community care. Sometimes hospital admission *is* needed and it can be hard to know when that is. I worry a lot about these kinds of things. Happily, this is not an issue today: Peter is doing well and has resumed his studies. He seems greatly relieved – and so am I.

–

Saturday 11 March

I keep thinking of a poem I read years ago but I cannot recall its title or author. It pops into my head as I'm doing my 'mindfulness of breathing' today. It goes something like: 'Tell me, what is god? He is the breath within the breath.' I know the line comes from a Sufi poem and, checking online, I find that my memory of the quote is almost correct. It is: 'Kabir says: Student, tell me, what is God? He is the breath inside the breath.' Kabir (1440–1518) was an Indian poet, mystic and philosopher.

I recall dipping into a book of his poems some years ago. I've no idea where my Kabir book is now. In true Buddhist spirit, I must not crave or grasp, but I would still like to read the full poem so I go searching for the book. I do not find it. There's probably a message there. The version I find online lacks the magic of the version I recall reading in the book. It is, as it were, *unsatisfactory*, or, in Buddhist terms, *duhkha*. The magic is lost in the past.

I go to bed.

Sunday 12 March

I've been thinking again about this month's theme, the cessation of suffering. This, the third noble truth, envisions a place beyond suffering, saying that such a place exists and it is possible to get there. Meditation is a key part of the journey according to Buddhism, but other activities matter too, especially if they declutter the mind and help one to focus on the essence of the present moment. In this context, I greatly admire the absorbed, selfless, almost meditative state achieved by certain artists and musicians in full flow and their utter immersion in the passing moment.

I go to a concert by the Gloaming in the elegant National Concert Hall. It's a lovely evening: crisp, dry and full of life. The Gloaming are an astonishing group of musicians. It is difficult to describe the Gloaming's music but it finds its deepest roots in Irish tradition and links this with jazz, contemporary classical and experimental music in all kinds of exciting ways. I've seen them play a couple of times before, but this evening the musicians seem especially transported by their playing and the entire audience is transported with them. A splendid, splendid evening.

–

Monday 13 March

I am off work this week so I do my meditation nice and early, before a couple of hours working on some papers and essays. This is followed by a trip to the cinema to see *Elle*, starring Isabelle Huppert. This is a dark, dark movie, filled with violence and tension, hatred and exploitation. On the plus side, the street scenes of Paris are lovely and they remind me of my trip earlier this year. Happily, nothing else in the film reminds me of anything else in my life. And thank goodness for that.

Tuesday 14 March

Up early again, fifteen minutes' meditation, then a couple of hours' work. At lunchtime I pop into a seminar about medical humanities in Trinity and then onward to the cinema for *The Viceroy's House*. The film depicts the end of British rule in India and the birth of India and Pakistan as independent countries. There is a great deal of melodrama but also much to savour. I'm interested in India since my first research trip there last year and I hope to go again later this year. India is big, different, far away and very interesting. They have new mental health legislation that is ambitious, progressive and quite fascinating because human rights in mental health is one of my key research interests.

–

Wednesday 15 March

Okay, so my week off is not really delivering the concentrated meditation sessions I had hoped for, but I am sticking to my fifteen minutes per day, spending only a couple of hours writing and going to the cinema *a lot*. That will have to be enough for now.

I spend the afternoon at the movies watching *Loving*, about Mildred and Richard Loving who were involved in a 1967 US Supreme Court decision invalidating state laws prohibiting interracial marriage. The film is very moving and I leave the cinema in reflective, sombre mood.

–

Thursday 16 March

I attend an early-morning silent meditation. It is a quiet, gentle hour. My thoughts amble off in odd directions, but come back more or less at my bidding. I seem to regard the 'me' who retrieves my wandering thoughts as somehow separate from the thoughts themselves. I'm not certain that makes sense.

I walk by the canal, which is its usual serene self. Even a scuttling rat does not seem out of place. Buddhism teaches us to respect all sentient beings and to cherish all forms of life, even rats.

Friday 17 March

St Patrick's Day. Up early, fifteen minutes' meditation and a couple of hours on the computer before the household moves into action. We go to see the parade. It's bitterly cold. I remember marching in the parade as a child and playing the tin whistle, then various brass instruments, in the school band. Add in several years of piano lessons and you would almost think I was musical. I am not.

–

Saturday 18 March

I am very fond of statues and images of Buddha even though I know virtually nothing about Buddhist iconography. I have a book on Buddhist art I dip into, especially when I'm trying to figure out the symbolism of Buddha's various postures. I have particular fondness for a wooden figure I picked up several years ago of Buddha meditating in perfect symmetry. It's especially calming and the wood has a nice organic feel to it.

I am most unlike Buddha. I am distracted and restless but I stick with the meditating. It's getting easier and that hour I spent with the meditation group two mornings ago was helpful. I must make time for it again.

–

Sunday 19 March

This month I'm rereading one of the most astonishing books I've ever come across, *Pure Heart, Enlightened Mind* by Maura O'Halloran. Maura was an Irish-American Zen Buddhist monk. Her book is essentially a meditation diary that she kept during her time in Japan, along with some other documents. It's fascinating.

Maura was educated in Dublin and trained as a Zen monk in Japan. After three years she was given the Buddhist name of 'Soshin-san', which means 'pure heart, enlightened mind'. Two months later, she died in a traffic accident in Thailand. I read Maura's diary many years ago and was deeply moved by it. I've given it to several people over the years along with *Soisín*, a CD inspired by Maura's story by the Irish group Kila. Luka Bloom has also written a song about Maura: the cover of his CD *Between the Mountain and the Moon* shows prayer flags at Dzogchen Beara, the incredible Tibetan Buddhist centre on the Beara Peninsula in West Cork, which I have happily visited in the past. In 2002 Alan Gilsenan directed *Maura's Story*, an amazing film filled with insights about Maura's life. Her diaries and writings provide a fascinating account of her story and the documentary complements the diaries perfectly.

I reread parts of Maura's diaries this month and think of her a good deal. She is a strong, gentle presence.

I've been to Japan, but I've never travelled to northern Japan to see the statue in Maura's honour, at the temple where she studied. I am told that part of the inscription reads: 'She is given the posthumous name of Great Enlightened Lady, of the same heart and mind as the great Teacher Buddha.' That sounds right.

I hope to visit someday. But for today, I dismiss all thoughts of travel to Japan. I sit and try to focus on the present moment, right here, right now. That is all there is: the present moment.

I have mixed success.

–

Monday 20 March
I am very distracted in my meditation today.

I see Peter again. His parents come along too, asking questions about schizophrenia. This is good. They speak to me at some length and it seems they recognise that Peter is much better than he was and that he continues to improve, but still they worry. I talk with Peter and his family, focusing on the nature of Peter's symptoms, the role of medication and other therapies, the advisability of avoiding cannabis and other drugs and steps to be taken in the event of any future deterioration in mental health.

I really feel for families in these situations. They have a lot of new information to absorb but I'm always hugely impressed by their resourcefulness when the condition and its treatment are explained. Once they are properly involved, the vast majority of families offer a level of understanding and support that takes my breath away. I guess I'm talking about love.

–

Tuesday 21 March

After a woeful night's sleep (awake from 4 am), I head off for an hour of silent meditation. I cycle along the canal on another glorious morning: cold, dry and astonishingly bright. The cycle path is crowded with people heading directly to their workplaces, but I soon veer off to my meditation sit. The high-ceilinged room is cool, bright and calming. The hour feels long due to my lack of sleep, but I do my best and feel better for it afterwards.

Then I cycle to work, uphill and into the wind. It is a most vigorous start to any day. The cycle reminds me of the time I tried swimming in the sea every morning before work, many years ago when I lived in Galway. I thought a daily swim would make me more energetic but it did the exact opposite: I was perpetually exhausted, forever nodding off to sleep mid-morning in work. I abandoned the idea after a few weeks. Here's hoping my meditation habit is more sustainable.

–

Wednesday 22 March

It never fails to astonish me when I open my eyes after meditating to find that Trixie has joined me. Googling around for Buddhist cat stories, I discover that there is a book called *The Dalai Lama's Cat*. I'm not certain that our cat is especially enlightened but she does seem very calm and is almost certainly further along the spiritual path than I am.

–

Thursday 23 March

Buddha: 'Whatever is not yours: let go of it. Your letting go of it will be for your long-term happiness and benefit.' Yes, yes, OK.

Friday 24 March

Another stunning day. I cycle in crisp sunshine to the silent meditation sit. I attend twice this week – that's pretty good for me! It's a lovely place, powerful and gentle.

When meditating at home, I sit squarely on a chair. Here I kneel on two meditation cushions with my knees on the mat. This is a good position for beginners such as me although it is not quite as solid as the lotus position. But, like many people, I find the lotus position causes excruciating pain and there is absolutely no point in that.

The hour passes briskly in the light-filled room. I'm finding it easier to let intrusive, babbling thoughts subside gently, rather than forcing them out of my mind. And it's a really perfect day for a positive frame of mind: cool, sunny, Friday.

–

Saturday 25 March

I have, of all the unlikely things for me to do, joined a gym: I actually joined several months ago for the swimming lessons, which I duly did. And while I attended the lessons I did not practise between them and therefore learned only a small amount. That was my second go at lessons and my second time to fail to practise. At least I do not sink but neither am I a strong swimmer. I think the problem is that I don't like swimming although I feel it's something I should be able to do better. Perhaps next time round I will be entranced by the magic of it, practise and become more devoted? That seems unlikely.

Right now I'm determined to give the gym a try, so my fifteen minutes of meditation today is followed by twenty minutes on a tread-mill and some stretches. I'd never stepped inside a gym until today. It's filled with athletic young people, exercising intently. There is constant music to keep everyone pumped up and active. It is a most peculiar place and I don't know if I like it or not.

Sunday 26 March

I go to see *The Secret Scripture*, based on the novel by Sebastian Barry. I loved the novel, not least because it concerns the history of psychiatry (one of my interests) and portrays a contemporary psychiatrist as being generally humane and reasonable. The sadness of institutional life is especially well portrayed, as are the possibility of rebirth and – consistent with this month's theme in my meditation project – the possibility of an end to suffering, despite a lifetime of isolation.

I often reflect on the extent to which today's mental health services have moved away from their institutional, asylum-based past. Do people now become institutionalised in their own homes, attending services but only in a repetitive, institutional pattern? Or has there been real change? These kinds of thoughts often trouble me but I console myself that an awareness of these risks might be a good step towards diminishing or avoiding them. Here's hoping.

–

Monday 27 March

The internet is full of guides to meditation: the simpler they are, the better. Too much instruction is a distraction. Too many books, CDs and websites function only as obstacles. It is best to pick one very simple set of instructions, establish a sustainable pace and commit to practice. I honour my commitment to fifteen minutes meditation per day and also manage to cycle to and from work, making today a good day.

–

Tuesday 28 March

I am on call again, meaning that I spend much of the evening in the hospital and take calls during the night from the hospital team, joining them in the emergency department or on the ward if needed. These circumstances, with one ear out for the phone at all times, are less than ideal for meditating. Nonetheless I plough on.

Wednesday 29 March

This morning is glorious and sunny and I cycle along the canal to my one-hour silent meditation sit. I'm doing a lot better attending this session over the past fortnight and it is proving very beneficial. There are three 'jewels' in Buddhism: the Buddha himself, the *dharma* (the teachings of the Buddha and the truth he understood) and the *sangha*. The *sangha* is the community of people with whom we practise and with whom we share our lives. All are essential.

—

Thursday 30 March

There is a quotation that crops across religious and spiritual traditions in various forms: 'You should sit in meditation for twenty minutes a day, unless you are too busy – then you should sit for an hour.' It sounds glib but it's probably true.

—

Friday 31 March

Today marks the end of month three of my year-long meditation project. I am now a quarter of the way through. What have I learned so far?

First, it *is* possible to find time to meditate every day, despite everything that comes crowding in. Second, gyms are very strange places, but not necessarily unpleasantly so. We will see what happens there (although the overwhelming likelihood is that I will never return to it). Third, the only discernible benefit from my meditation practice so far is that I've become a more reflective about my moment-to-moment states of mind and this will hopefully decrease the amount of time I spend in an irritated, unfocused state. This is easily good enough to justify the time and effort I've put in so far. Fourth, I still don't understand the cat.

I meditate for fifteen minutes.

And then I eat some really delicious cake. This month: an almond slice, with ill-defined goo in the middle.

» Meditation, Mindfulness and Mental Health

To 'meditate' is to exercise the mind in contemplation or focus the mind on a subject in a concentrated, contemplative or religious manner. Meditation and contemplative practices play a substantive role in many spiritual, religious and psychological traditions. In recent years there has been an upsurge of research interest in the effects of meditation on the brain and the possible use of meditation in the management of a range of physical and mental illnesses. There has also been a substantial increase in public interest in contemplative practice both as a method to manage psychological symptoms, such as anxiety and depression, and a way to maintain mental health.

» Meditation and the Brain

Meditative and contemplative practices involve several coordinated brain functions performed simultaneously, often over a prolonged period or on repeated occasions. There is long-standing evidence that practising meditation has significant effects on the way the brain works including increased blood flow in certain parts of the brain (Newberg *et al.*, 2003) and changes in electrical brain-wave patterns (Lutz *et al*, 2004).

These findings suggest that prolonged or long-term meditation may have sustained effects on the physiology of the brain – effects which persist even when the individual is no longer meditating. Meditation also has significant, sustained effects on individuals who are not long-term meditators but just engage in short-term practice. Individuals who are not habitual meditators but attend an eight-week training programme in mindfulness meditation show significant changes in brain activation and improvements in their immune systems for fighting infections (Davidson *et al.*, 2003).

Any model integrating these and other research findings into a single, unified theory of how meditation affects the brain is hampered by the small numbers of subjects in existing studies, the diversity of physiological measures examined and general limitations on current understandings of brain structure and function. Nonetheless, Austin (2006) has attempted to provide an integrated model that combines neuroscientific findings with the psychological and experiential correlates of meditative practice, especially from the Zen (or *Ch'an*) tradition of Buddhism. While Austin's model is both insightful and provocative, there is clearly a need for more basic neuroscientific research and psychological investigation of the effects of meditation.

» *Meditation and Mental Health*

Meditation and contemplative prayer are accorded substantial value in many spiritual and religious schools, especially those with strong monastic traditions. Roman Catholicism, for example, incorporates elements of solitary living, individual prayer and prolonged, silent contemplation. While research into the effects of contemplative practice on the brain has tended to focus on long-term Buddhist meditators (Lutz *et al.*, 2004), there is evidence of similar effects in Roman Catholic practitioners of contemplative prayer, such as Franciscan nuns (Newberg *et al.*, 2003).

The Buddhist tradition is fundamentally centred on the practice of meditation to produce calm (*amatha*) and meditation to produce insight (*vipa yan*) (Gethin, 1998). Buddhism also has a particularly intricate literature on the psychological correlates of contemplative practice: the *Abhidharma* or 'higher teaching' of Buddhism is essentially devoted to a systematic description of all possible states of mind and cognitive functions, many of which are presented in association with the levels of meditative attainment in which they are experienced. Clear understanding and personal experience of these mental states are essential prerequisites for spiritual advancement and the development of insight.

The reasons why various traditions value contemplative practice vary significantly: in Roman Catholicism contemplative prayer is directed at a specific God, often with the purpose of praise or intercession, while in Buddhism, meditation is not directed at any specific deity but aimed at producing individual enlightenment. In most spiritual traditions, however, contemplative prayer or meditation is seen as a positive, progressive element within an individual's broader spiritual practice.

In terms of mental health, there is evidence that 'spiritual meditation' is superior to both 'secular meditation' and 'secular' relaxation techniques in reducing anxiety, improving mood, enhancing spiritual health and increasing tolerance of pain (Wachholtz and Pargament, 2005). This is consistent with the facts that individuals attending mental health services consistently identify spirituality as a significant factor in determining mental health and spirituality is significantly correlated with higher global quality of life, hope and sense of community (Bellamy *et al.*, 2007).

» Meditation and Mental Illness

There is a growing literature examining the possible role of meditative practices (for example, mindfulness) in the management of specific mental illnesses such as anxiety disorders, depression, alcohol misuse, substance misuse, post-traumatic stress disorder and psychosomatic disorders. Most such studies tend to be based on opportunistic samples, include small numbers of participants and have sharply limited generalisability outside the study settings.

Anxiety disorders are the most commonly studied disorders in this context, with a moderate number of studies examining the effects of mindfulness meditation, meditation-based stress reduction and transcendental meditation. A review of the existing research, however, highlighted a marked paucity of high-quality, randomised controlled trials of meditation therapy for anxiety disorders, with only two studies qualifying for inclusion in the review (Krisanaprakornkit *et al.*, 2006). In addition, the authors noted that drop-out rates for research studies appeared to be high, adverse effects of meditation had not been reported and further study was needed before conclusions could be drawn.

There are even fewer randomised controlled trials of meditation for other disorders, further highlighting the need for systematic investigation of the effects of meditation for specific mental illnesses. In addition, despite a long-standing association between certain forms of meditation (for example, Zen) and certain forms of psychotherapy (for example, psychoanalysis) (Fromm *et al.*, 1960; Epstein, 2007), there remains a similar need for further systematic considerations of the precise role of meditation in the analytic context.

In the meantime there are scattered reports of varying levels of rigour suggesting the usefulness of specific meditative practices in specific groups of patients: mindfulness meditation, for example, may help alleviate depressive symptoms in women with fibromyalgia (Sephton *et al.*, 2007). There is also a research review examining the possible benefits of meditation therapies for attention deficit/hyperactivity disorder (ADHD) as suggested by small studies of the use of yoga and meditation strategies in children with ADHD (Krisanaprakornkit *et al.*, 2007).

At present, however, there is insufficient evidence to support the systematic use of meditation therapy for any specific mental illness, apart from preventing recurrence of depression in certain patients. This situation may change in future years in response to further study of the neuroscience of meditation, more randomised controlled trials and systematic reviews (especially in relation to anxiety disorders), continued emphasis on spirituality among mental-health-service users and sustained public interest in forms of psychological therapy that focus on mental wellness rather than illness.

In particular, recent years have seen social-policymakers increasingly focus on happiness as a societal goal and this trend is likely to deepen interest in psychological therapies that appear to advance this goal while remaining acceptable to the public (Layard, 2005). On this basis, meditation, with its lengthy history in myriad cultures, is likely to attract increasing attention in the years to come.

April

—

A POSSIBLE WAY FORWARD

In which I continue to meditate with grim determination but generally unsatisfactory results. I see squirrels. Trixie continues to puzzle and enlighten. This month also brings a focus on how to overcome *duhkha*, or unsatisfactoriness, by following the noble eightfold path of Buddhist tradition. This is not easy. I ruminate on sleep, dreams, Indian sculpture, any number of movies, psychotherapy, the Buddhist teachings of 'dependent arising' and 'no self' and the origins of Zen. In short, I do everything to avoid real commitment to meditation but somehow manage to sustain my fifteen minutes per day. Blindly, I stagger on.

Saturday 1 April

Right, then. Month four. Here we go. Fifteen minutes' meditation on a dank, damp day. Done.

–

Sunday 2 April

There are many online guides on how to meditate. Just google 'meditation instructions' and you'll come up with thousands of websites offering advice. Much of it is excellent, focusing on timing, posture, breathing, thoughts and various other aspects of meditation. Sometimes, though, it's good to ignore all the detailed advice, position yourself comfortably in a chair with your back relatively straight and just sit.

–

Monday 3 April

Early this morning, I open my eyes after I sit and I see a squirrel on the road in front of the house. Squirrels are frequent visitors where we live in Dublin. Trixie and the occasional fox discourage them, so it's especially lovely to spot one running about today, filled with energy and curiosity. A small glimpse of wildlife in the city.

–

Tuesday 4 April

This month's theme in my meditation project is the fourth noble truth of Buddhism, which is how to overcome *duhkha* or unsatisfactoriness. This truth concerns the precise ways in which suffering can be overcome and *nirvana* achieved. It refers to the noble eightfold path, based on the three key principles of wisdom, moral virtue and meditation. As with the four noble truths, Buddhist literature contains many more detailed accounts of the eightfold path. Each element of the eightfold path will be touched upon over the next eight months of my meditation project (if I manage to keep going that long).

I meditate on the three key principles of wisdom, moral virtue and meditation. Meditating about meditation is curiously circular. I do it anyway.

Wednesday 5 April
The wireless cackles.
A leaf falls down. Is not a
plum tree beautiful?

—

Thursday 6 April
I like to sleep but am not good at it. I cannot sleep on trains or airplanes, in cars, in front of the television or anywhere other than bed. In bed, I fall asleep readily but wake early, at five or six am, and rarely return to sleep. My dreams seem random but last year in India a combination of jet lag, anti-malaria medication and general excitement gave me glorious, intense, technicolour dreams. The only other thing that affected my dreams so dramatically in the past was meditation. When I used to meditate for an hour a week some years ago I developed very vivid dreams that were neither good nor bad but always strangely comforting. This has not happened this time round.

—

Friday 7 April
Asian culture fascinates me. Before last year's trip to India, I was already very taken by Victor's Way, an Indian sculpture garden near Dublin, just north of the village of Roundwood in County Wicklow. The garden is thoughtfully laid out but not manicured. It is filled with enormous and surprising sculptures of Hindu deities such as Ganesh and Shiva and figures such as 'Fasting Buddha', 'Awakening', 'Split Man' and 'Nirvana Man'. The entrance, Victoria's Gate, is unique and astonishing, as befits such an unusual, unexpectedly spiritual place. It is an excellent spot for a contemplative walk.

Saturday 8 April

I wake up in Cork where I am to attend a meeting at University College Cork about Ireland's new mental capacity legislation. My hotel room is wonderful: high above the river, looking down onto the water and right across Cork city. It is easy to meditate here, as it often is in inspiring surroundings. And today is a perfect day: dry, crisp, cool. After the meeting I spend the afternoon driving back to Dublin and arrive in time to attend *Private Lives* at the Gate. I like the play a lot: the theatre is almost full and the actors are clearly on form. I arrive home at 11 pm, profoundly exhausted.

–

Sunday 9 April

Buddha: 'Understanding is the heartwood of well-spoken words.' True, for sure, but not so easy to achieve.

–

Monday 10 April

Today brings two movies, *Personal Shopper* and *I Am Not Your Negro*. The latter is an extraordinary film. I leave the cinema in a daze. Walking though Temple Bar, nothing seems real; it's as if everyone is pretending or acting or has been replaced by other people. I feel like I'm watching the world go past on television. This is a feeling I often experience after a good movie: it is a mild version of the 'derealisation' (things not seeming real) and 'depersonalisation' (people, including yourself, not feeling real) that patients sometimes describe. They usually report this as an upsetting experience whereas what I experience today is settling, rather than disquieting, and ultimately peaceful.

Tuesday 11 April

Busy day: I have an engagement in Trinity in the morning and then drive to Kenmare in Kerry. The weather is stunning and I listen to Imelda May's *Life Love Flesh Blood* on the way down: it's splendid, full of energy and life. I meditate somewhere around lunchtime but it's the music that affects me most today.

I arrive in Kenmare late in the evening: the main street is quiet with just two or three tourists looking in shop windows. When I reach my accommodation, I'm told that there was a young deer standing in the grass outside the houses just a few moments ago. A group of children are very excited and their parents struggle to contain them. We take a look in the trees and the fields beyond, but the deer has vanished. I make tea.

–

Wednesday 12 April

This month's theme – how to overcome *duhkha* – is rooted in the three principles of wisdom, moral virtue and meditation. I'm not certain I have much of any of these, but I will nonetheless focus on each element of the eightfold path over the coming months. I wonder does thinking about these eight virtues in this clear, enunciated fashion actually help achieve them?

I like the word 'right'. It suggests that some things are right and other things are wrong. Not everything is relative. Right and wrong exist. They are actual things. And the examples that make up the eight-fold path are not exactly controversial. Who could possibly object to 'right speech'? But what, exactly, does 'right speech' mean? And how does one achieve it?

Thursday 13 April

We visit Dzogchen Beara, the Buddhist centre on the Beara Peninsula in West Cork. It is the long-term retreat centre for Rigpa, an international network of Buddhist centres. As we drive in, there is a marmalade cat fast asleep in the middle of the road. The cat is entirely untroubled by the risk of passing cars: this is a Buddhist centre, after all, filled with respect for sentient beings. The meditation room is calm and calming, with an expansive view over the sea. As we leave, an emu wanders down the road. Has it escaped from an emu farm? Are there emu farms in Cork? Or did we imagine it?

–

Friday 14 April

Sign on a shop front: 'Vacancy exists. Enquire within.' Indeed!

–

Saturday 15 April

So many quotes online are attributed to Buddha, often accompanied by heated discussions about the 'true' origins of the quotes. One of the most ubiquitous is: 'Holding on to anger is like grasping a hot coal with the intent of harming another; you end up getting burned.' There is much debate about where this particular quote comes from, but regardless of its origin it has always seemed to me that there is a great deal of truth in it. Anger is hard to avoid and exceptionally difficult to let go of when it arises. But anger goes nowhere and I increasingly think that being angry is the opposite of being strong.

–

Sunday 16 April

Zen is a school of Buddhism that originated in China and has proven especially iconic. For many people, Zen is the epitome of Buddhism even though it is only one of various schools to have emerged over past centuries. Zen is best known for its focus on self-control, meditation, direct understanding and interaction with a teacher. I attended one strict Zen meditation session in Dublin many years ago. After sitting in meditation we practised *kinhin* (walking meditation), taking slow steps in a clockwise direction, holding our hands in particular ways and breathing according to a specific rhythm. It was very strict and formalised. It was not for me and I did not return. I am a Zen failure.

–

Monday 17 April

Back to Dublin today after a lovely Easter weekend in Galway. The drive is peaceful and I collect Trixie from the cattery. She is glad to see me but seems slightly disturbed as she often does after a period apart. She sits with me quietly for the fifteen minutes, but she's still not quite right. Or perhaps it's me who's not quite right? I wonder what she thinks.

–

Tuesday 18 April

Back to work today. I'm busy sorting out various matters after my ten days away, but everything gets done in the end. I see a man with a severe phobia in the afternoon. We don't often see people with phobic fears of things any more. I wonder why? Perhaps they just don't come to see psychiatrists?

This man has tussaphobia – a severe phobia of coughing. He goes to enormous lengths to avoid coughing and has to go through an elaborate ritual of changing and washing his clothes when he does cough. But it's even worse if someone else coughs. If he is in a room and someone coughs, he must leave the room at once (often causing acute social embarrassment) and go through his changing and washing routine as soon as possible in a 'place of safety'.

As we talk it is clear that there is a strong obsessive-compulsive element to all of this, as this man's fundamental anxiety takes several different shapes: avoiding coughs, obsessional thinking about coughing, compulsively changing and washing his clothes. The current approach to this kind of dilemma focuses on psychological therapy looking at the feelings, thoughts and behaviours that reinforce anxieties, obsessions and compulsions. Some people also benefit from antidepressant medication (anxiety and depression are often indistinguishable) but this man is very keen on psychological therapy alone, which is fine.

Thinking about cases like this, I often reflect on how these distressing patterns of feeling, thinking and behaving develop and are sustained. Do they always have initial triggering events? Or do they just start randomly and then accumulate over time, reinforced through simple habit?

As well as organising psychological therapy, I feel that this man might benefit from some contemplative practice. He does not seem ready for the 'clear mind' required in meditation so yoga might be useful as it focuses on mind *and* body. I suggest it to him but he seems to think I'm joking. For now, though, we arrange psychological therapy and I will see him again soon to see how things are going.

I go for a walk when I get home. It's a contemplative evening, warm and summery. I notice that I cough twice during dinner, which is unusual for me. Is my subconscious telling me something? If so, I have no idea what.

–

Wednesday 19 April
This month's theme suggests I should be reflecting on wisdom, moral virtue and meditation and using these to overcome *duhkha*. Today, however, I spend a lot more time discussing future research projects in the area of mental health law rather than living in the present moment. But that – planning future projects – *is* what I'm doing right now. Surely focusing on that *is* focusing on the present moment? Or is that argument too circular? I realise that argument does not make sense and it's important to focus on the present moment in a less reflexive, simpler, more straightforward way. Yes, that is infinitely better: less cognitive, more experiential, more direct.

Thursday 20 April

It takes three months to establish a new habit. I've been meditating every day for over three months now and it is still not a strong habit. I still need to seek out space in the day to meditate and defend it vigorously from other pressing matters – the myriad distractions of life. A quick Google search tells me, however, that there is actually wide variation in how long it takes to form a new habit. But is that true? Can we google 'How reliable is Google?'

–

Friday 21 April

Busy day at work. I try to be mindful. I fail.

–

Saturday 22 April

We go for a spectacular cycle on the Old Rail Trail, a dedicated greenway for walking and cycling from Mullingar to Athlone in County Westmeath. It is 40 kilometres each way and makes for a contemplative day on the bicycle. We meet very few people but a great many cows, sheep, horses, hens, birds and, just outside Mullingar, a pine marten. The pine marten moves very quickly into the bushes by the canal but we are delighted to see it. I've never seen a pine marten in the wild before. It is a genuinely magical moment.

After more than 80 kilometres on the bike, I need to acknowledge the fortifying, restorative ministrations of Mr Wong's Chinese Restaurant at the Mullingar Park Hotel. It is a perfect post-cycle, post-pine marten dining venue.

–

Sunday 23 April

Trixie puzzles and enlightens in equal measure. She is very Zen. She sits with me. She yawns and goes to sleep. She is not a Zen failure.

Monday 24 April

I devote some time to this month's book, *Psychotherapy Without the Self* by Mark Epstein, a collection of papers and essays dealing with such diverse themes as meditation and narcissism, forms of emptiness, pitfalls on the spiritual path and – my favourite – 'attention in analysis', looking in detail at the therapist's use of attention during psychological therapy. There is also a very insightful essay on the use of psychiatric medication in conjunction with meditation for some people. Often a combination of approaches is best: one size does not fit all.

–

Tuesday 25 April

I've always liked the idea of 'understanding' in Buddhism, the idea of 'seeing things as they truly are'. Much of this 'understanding' centres on the Buddhist teaching of 'dependent arising', which refers to the idea that all phenomena arise, abide and pass away because of specific causes and conditions. As a result, everything is dependent on everything else and, contrary to appearances, nothing has autonomous, lasting substance. All phenomena are therefore without essence or under-lying substance *in and of themselves*. They are empty. These phenomena include the 'self', which is also without substance, permanence or inde-pendent existence. 'We' are intrinsically networked phenomena, pres-ences dispersed across a system, ghosts in a machine.

In other words, for every phenomenon (including the self) there is a collection of causes and conditions that give rise to it: these (including the self) are in a state of continuous change. Therefore, there is no fixed or identifiable self, only the passing, changing impression of one.

Buddhism does not exactly teach that there is *no* self. Clearly, I myself am typing these words and you yourself are reading them. Rather, Buddhism teaches that the idea of 'self' has an illusory fixedness about it, a misleading appearance of substance and permanence that leads us to believe that the 'self' is an autonomous, lasting, defined entity. It is not. Like everything else, the 'self' is dependent on a range of other circumstances and conditions in order to exist; it is constantly changing and therefore lacks the substance that we routinely attribute to it.

This is a very optimistic teaching in Buddhist tradition. Change is the only constant so the problems of today may well be gone tomorrow and the positive actions of today can influence the future in a positive way (*karma*). In addition, the suffering (*duhkha*) that one 'self' experiences is continuous with the suffering of others, because we are all a single, unified phenomenon, without distinction between artificially constructed 'selves'.

This is a powerful argument in favour of compassion towards all, including one's 'self'. Your suffering is continuous with mine – and so is your happiness.

–

Wednesday 26 April

That being said, I'm still not at all certain that I've made much progress, if any, with this month's theme, the fourth noble truth, which is how to overcome *duhkha* or unsatisfactoriness. I certainly have not overcome unsatisfactoriness myself and I definitely have not achieved *nirvana*. Still, I have meditated steadily enough, chipping along gamely. Perhaps that is enough for now.

I again see the man with the coughing phobia from last week. He now has an appointment date with a psychological therapist the week after next and he looks forward to that. He has researched the therapeutic value of yoga on the internet and has decided that my suggestion that he try yoga in order to help reduce his anxiety was a serious suggestion after all. I'm delighted.

–

Thursday 27 April

I wake up in Limerick. I am in a good hotel: I find mid-range hotel rooms oddly soothing and, on my occasional work trips, they are pleasingly solitary for writing papers or sitting quietly. There is much to be said for sitting quietly.

Friday 28 April

I conduct a seminar about the history of psychiatry at the University of Limerick. There are birds singing everywhere on the north side of the campus. As I leave, I pass the hall where I saw the Dalai Lama in April 2011: it's a long time ago now but I remember the event fondly. And as I drive home I listen to a superb CD, *Foundry Folk Songs* by the Sons of Southern Ulster. It's not exactly meditative or Buddhist but it helps with the journey.

–

Saturday 29 April

Waiting for Godot in the Abbey Theatre. I have not seen *Godot* for many years and it is (again) astonishing. I really do not tire of Beckett. I'm still reading two pages of his novels every night and enjoying them greatly. I write about Beckett a little more in 'Ego, id and Ireland' (p. 187).

My essay is primarily concerned with Sigmund Freud, the father of psychoanalysis. In 2010, for reasons that remain obscure even to me, I decided to read all twenty-four volumes of the *Standard Edition of the Complete Psychological Works of Sigmund Freud*, at the rate of one volume per year. I write an essay each year in the *Irish Medical Times*. 'Ego, id and Ireland' reflects a little more on that project and on Beckett.

Reading over what I've written in this journal just now, I see that I am very fond of projects, perhaps pathologically so: reading one volume of Freud per year; reading two pages of Beckett per day; meditating for fifteen minutes every day for a year (hopefully). But there's no point getting mired in too much self-reflection about this, especially if the 'self' in the term 'self-reflection' does not really exist!

–

Sunday 30 April

Today's meditation sit marks my arrival one-third way of the way through my one-year meditation project. What have I achieved so far? I've meditated every day for four months and, for me, that is certainly an achievement in itself. Has it had any effect? I don't think so, at least not in any major way. I am, perhaps, more reflective about my mental states, but that might equally come from keeping this journal rather than meditation itself. I was never much good at keeping a journal until now.

It is perhaps time to get more serious about meditating and to focus less on the journal. I reflect on these thoughts as I take a short walk by the canal after work.

It is a pleasant evening and I eat some cake.

This month it's Battenberg, a sponge cake with jam, coated with marzipan. When I was young, this was my favourite treat. It was known as 'chapel windows' because the yellow and pink sponge resemble stained-glass windows in a church. Forty years later, I still love it.

THE NOBLE EIGHTFOLD PATH

—

May

—

RIGHT VIEW

In which I go to see yet more movies, think about the Buddhist concept of 'right view' and try to keep on meditating. Trixie continues to perplex me, but in a companionable way. This month also brings more nuggets of wisdom attributed to Buddha, early morning meditation (although not nearly enough) and many, many distractions that are ever more elaborate ways to avoid focusing more deeply on meditating. Onward, onward.

Monday 1 May

It's a Bank Holiday weekend so I see three movies at the IFI (an excellent start to any month): *Suntan*, a Greek film about a doctor who fails to act his age; *Lady Macbeth*, a dark, compelling film; and *Handsome Devil*, an Irish coming-of-age movie set in a boys' boarding school. *Suntan*, probably the least accomplished of today's three films, lingers with me the longest, possibly because it concerns a male doctor in his forties, even though Dr Kostis's situation and life choices bear no relation to mine.

–

Tuesday 2 May

Turning more seriously to my meditation project again, I decide that this month I need to focus more on the experiential aspect of meditating and reflect more clearly on my contemplative experiences in this journal: in other words, I should write more about the realities of contemplative practice and less about looking things up online, the cat, seeing movies and general chit chat. I have a ceaselessly wandering mind.

–

Wednesday 3 May

This month's theme is 'right view', the first element of the noble eight-fold path of Buddhist thought. The noble eightfold path is a set of guidelines about how best to think and behave in the world in order to reduce suffering, both one's own and that of others.

So what, exactly, is right view? Essentially, it means seeing things as they really are, free of delusion and interpretation, free of distortion and artifice. It is sometimes described as seeing the true nature of reality (including the 'self'), moving beyond labels and names, understanding and accepting the outer and inner nature of phenomena as they truly are (not how we imagine or initially perceive them to be) and – critically – recognising that actions have consequences (*karma*).

Cultivating right view invariably involves sitting quietly with reality and letting the surrounding dust and clamour settle, so as to reveal a clear view of unvarnished truth. It is like looking at a glass of water and waiting patiently for the sediment to settle, leaving only a crystal-clear body of water that demonstrates the true qualities and transparency of water in its purest form.

The 'self' is like the water in this analogy, only more so. If we sit quietly and non-judgementally for long enough, the self will not only become transparent, it will disappear.

–

Thursday 4 May

I try to maintain 'right view' all day. It's not easy, but making the effort certainly makes a difference. Perhaps that's what matters most.

I note that so far in this diary most of the clinical cases I have discussed have had demonstrable diagnoses: depression, panic disorder, schizophrenia and so forth. In truth, though, many – possibly most – of the people I see as a psychiatrist present with complicated mixtures of different symptoms that do not adhere to any particular pattern. Many have had difficult childhoods compounded by poverty and social disadvantage and now combined with new stressors: unemployment, bereavement, crime and other forms of loss or trauma. A great number either use cannabis habitually or use alcohol excessively or both, and feel much better when they stop. But the great majority do not fit into any specific diagnostic category. Every person is different and much of the human suffering I see is shaped by adverse life circumstances and limited life choices rather than anything else.

–

Friday 5 May

I cycle along the canal to the early-morning silent meditation session. The meditation sit is its usual self: gentle, welcoming and restorative. My mind wanders a great deal.

I cycle to work for a long, busy day, before arriving home around 8.30 pm. Despite my exhaustion, I sleep poorly. It's peculiar how my renewed meditation practice this year has not affected my sleep or dreams, as it did some years ago. It could happen yet.

Saturday 6 May

The weekend! I'm up early and work on papers and other matters from 5.30 am to 9 am, when family life kicks in. It's a chilly, blowy day. Trixie is in an odd state. She sits with me in the early morning but then eyes me with distinct *froideur* before going out through the cat flap to do whatever she does when she goes out through the cat flap. That cat is a riddle, wrapped in a mystery, inside an enigma, covered with fur. I will never understand her. I expect she has a shrewd understanding of me.

–

Sunday 7 May

Right, so we hit a glitch today: I am so preoccupied with other things that I almost don't sit at all. I have a dim memory of a study someone did of a meditation programme in a prison, looking at why prisoners dropped out of meditating. The most common reason the prisoners gave was that they did not have the time.

–

Monday 8 May

Buddha: 'Pay no attention to the faults of others, things done or left undone by others. Consider only what by oneself is done or left undone.' I do not leave my meditation undone today!

–

Tuesday 9 May

There is another quote, also attributed to Buddha, that plays particularly on my mind today: 'What you think, you become. What you feel, you attract. What you imagine, you create.' I especially like the idea that 'what you think, you become' in the sense that the thoughts I routinely think *are* my cognitive identity. The things I do each day *are* my life. It all starts today. It is always starting today. I *am* what I do and think and feel today. That's me. That's who I am. It is a very sobering thought but it is also liberating.

Wednesday 10 May

The weather is glorious this week. I'm cycling around the city and arriving to work full of energy and sunshine and the like. I'm focused especially on some papers we're submitting for publication, relating chiefly to mental health legislation in Ireland and India. It's interesting work and very cognitive. It's all in my head. It's all about ideas and thinking and writing. I need to counterbalance this with some more cycling, meditating or even – wait for it! – a trip to the gym.

–

Thursday 11 May

Today is the day of my inaugural lecture as Professor of Psychiatry at Trinity College Dublin, a post I took up around a year ago. I am supposed to summarise my professional career to date and outline future plans. It is also a ceremonial occasion. This is not the kind of event that I usually enjoy so I need a little contemplative time.

In the lecture itself I focus on my key interests in epidemiology (the distribution of mental illness across the population), the law as it relates to mental health (in Ireland and India) and medical education (I like teaching). I've only ever been to one inaugural lecture so I'm not certain if I strike the right note, but it all seems to go fine in the end.

I'm ravenous after the event and the long day and just about manage to eat something quickly at home before collapsing into bed.

–

Friday 12 May

I'm up and about early today because my team is presenting at 'Grand Rounds' in Tallaght University Hospital at 8 am. Grand Rounds is a weekly event where the clinical staff get together and talk about recent cases of educational interest or other relevant topics. My team is talking about our research study, looking at mental capacity in advance of Ireland's new mental capacity legislation, the Assisted Decision-Making (Capacity) Act 2015. The new legislation is an exciting development that will offer new structures for supported decision-making for people whose mental capacity is impaired (for example, some people with dementia). The new legislation will help Ireland better accord with international human rights standards but will also require significant changes in health and social care. We have a good discussion on the topic.

–

Saturday 13 May
I am delighted that a busy week is over. Today is a quiet day: a little work in the early morning and a quick sit, followed by a day of family activity and a DVD in the evening, *The Lunchbox*. The movie is light and extremely pleasant.

–

Sunday 14 May
Psychiatry is an unusual profession. People are referred to me for highly personal and often private reasons, and they are expected to speak entirely openly to me – a complete stranger – about things they have never told anyone else and can barely even acknowledge themselves. The astonishing thing is that so many people are ready to open up in this way. They just do. As a result, it is a real privilege to have this role and this privilege counter-balances some of the stresses of the job: worries about risk, pressures of work, and the uncertainty that forms an invariable part of all good medical practice. I reflect on these themes today and on the unusual, fulfilling job that I am lucky enough to hold. And then I go home.

–

Monday 15 May
Fifteen minutes of reasonable meditation. It's impossible to force thoughts from the mind so the challenge lies in letting them drift away of their own accord. This is difficult because I'm often ready to concentrate while meditating, whereas what I need to do is in many ways the opposite – to relax and loosen my involvement with passing thoughts and feelings.

Tuesday 16 May

For my meditation project book this month I'm rereading *The Lady and the Monk: Four Seasons in Kyoto* by Pico Iyer. I read this book when it first appeared in 1991 and I loved it immediately. In truth, I commonly enjoy books about people who go to live somewhere else for a period and report back on their exploits, but I especially liked Iyer's sensitive, literary exploration of Japan and his particular focus on Buddhism.

Later, I enjoyed Iyer's travel writing and other books including *The Open Road: The Global Journey of the Fourteenth Dalai Lama* which was particularly interesting because Iyer knows the Dalai Lama and writes about him with sensitivity and insight. Indeed, all of Iyer's writing is infused with a sort of translucent Buddhist sensibility, even when he's not discussing Buddhism.

But *The Lady and the Monk* remains my firm favourite: there is a crystal-clear quality to the prose that sets it well apart from most travelogues and a genuine engagement with Buddhism that differentiates it from some of the more superficial, self-aggrandising memoirs of contemplative practice. I dimly recall writing to Iyer many years ago to express my admiration for the book and him writing back, but I cannot find the letters, even in my dog-eared copy of *The Lady and the Monk*. Perhaps my memory is playing tricks on me? Not to worry: Buddhism teaches that permanence is an illusion anyway.

–

Wednesday 17 May

Busy day today. At work I see a woman with severe depression, a young man following an episode of self-harm, two people with anxiety disorders, and two people who are not so much mentally ill as deeply troubled by their life circumstances. They are both unemployed young men with traumatic pasts, both smoke cannabis daily and both have considered self-harm. I speak at some length with each of them and direct them to various community resources to augment the mental health services: drugs centres, employment supports and counselling services.

I hope they get on OK. There will be more people with similar problems tomorrow. And the next day. And the next.

–

Thursday 18 May

The early-morning meditation sit, is, as ever, a positive experience. For the first twenty minutes I focus with enthusiasm and then my mind wanders. I bring my thoughts gently back to my breath. The second twenty minutes are much more difficult: longer distractions, more difficulty controlling my thoughts and a kind of low-grade restlessness sets in. This is the most challenging phase. If I can manage simply to let this pass away (as it invariably does), then the final twenty minutes is the best period of all: quieter and steadier, albeit with a growing sadness that the hour is coming to an end and the world – with all its noise and care and worries – will soon come flooding in.

The clatter and clamour of morning time on Baggot Street is strangely pleasing today, though. Soothing, even. I spot delivery vans, commuters enjoying a last cup of coffee before work, people wandering around the street and tourists staring fixedly at their mobile phones. It all flows past. I seem to be more observant than I was, without the need to engage my thoughts fully in the hustle and bustle of life. Perhaps that is a benefit of meditation? I go to work.

–

Friday 19 May

Buddha: 'Should you find a wise critic to point out your faults, follow him as you would a guide to hidden treasure.' There's no shortage of critics, but how many are wise? And how can I tell which are wise and which are not?

At work, I see Tanya, an eighteen-year old girl who routinely cuts herself with knives, blades and various other things. She is only slightly distressed by this. She has come along to see me today solely at her partner's request. At some level she knows there is a problem, but she is not quite ready to admit this. Tanya is frustrated that everyone sees the self-cutting as the key issue whereas she sees it as a symptom. We talk through her behaviour a little but shift focus quite quickly to her partner. Clearly, Tanya listened to her partner's advice to come to see me today. Why? And can Tanya see why her partner might be worried?

–

Saturday 20 May

I'm not certain what Trixie makes of meditative endeavours. She seems philosophical herself, although perhaps she is just sitting there. Maybe that's what meditation is? Sitting blankly, like the cat.

–

Sunday 21 May

I'm on call so I spend much of the day in the hospital, assessing people and working with the team. I also take calls during the night and go in if needed. Being on call can be intense, and today is long and busy. As usual, the 24-hour period brings a real mix of cases: people who have self-harmed and are treated in the emergency department before being referred to the psychiatry team; people who feel depressed and come to hospital in search of help; and parents bringing in their young adult children about whom they are concerned owing to unusual behaviour or distressing thoughts. The flow of cases presents a real challenge to meditation, even during lulls in activity. The challenge is by no means insurmountable but I need to get better at surmounting it!

–

Monday 22 May

More Buddha: 'I will not look at another's bowl, intent on finding fault: a training to be observed.' That is much easier said than done. Surely we are always looking 'at another's bowl, intent on finding fault'?

Tuesday 23 May

It is perhaps time to get this journal back on track, time to reconsider this month's theme in my meditation project: 'right view', the first element of the noble eightfold path. Right view means seeing things as they really are, free of delusion and interpretation, free of distortion and artifice. That is, seeing the true nature of reality, including the 'self', and really understanding that everything is transitory to its very core. And that all actions have consequences, good and bad.

This is easy to understand but difficult to implement. I suppose it means not becoming too attached to passing phenomena. But while this is all good and well for emotions such as anger and irritation, what about happiness? And while it is good and well for material objects that I don't really need, what about objects that I do need: bed, kettle, bicycle? I suppose it's a matter of degree: disproportionate attachment brings suffering, enlightened involvement does not.

I am troubled by such thoughts today.

–

Wednesday 24 May

Yet more Buddha: 'Should a person do good, let him do it again and again. Let him find pleasure therein, for blissful is the accumulation of good.' And blissful indeed is the weather today! I go for a cycle around Dublin's docklands: still quite devoid of traffic in places and full of unexpected open spaces, water and bridges. Just enough people around to remind me that I'm not alone on the planet, but not so many as to disturb my solitude.

–

Thursday 25 May

Another good week for movies. I see the re-released *Manhattan*, and *Frantz*, which focuses on a German woman whose fiancé is killed in World War I. The entire film conveys a powerful anti-war message, highly consistent with Buddhist teaching and with the values I'm trying to develop during this meditation project.

Friday 26 May

I have singularly failed to visit the gym regularly this year, managing only one or two episodes on the treadmill. I'm doing much better with my meditation but there is still great room for improvement all round. Must try harder.

—

Saturday 27 May

I have recommended mindfulness and yoga to many patients over the years. The recommendation is a little paradoxical because the skills required for mindfulness and yoga (concentration, focus and so forth) tend to be precisely those that the patients complain they do not have. As a result, they often say: 'But that's exactly what I *can't* do!'

In fact, that is the reason why mindfulness or yoga can prove so useful: the skills mindfulness and yoga work on are exactly the ones many patients need to work on too. Mindfulness or yoga classes offer a structured pathway to improvement and I've seen many people benefit greatly from them. And while many patients have not followed my advice over the years, I've seen no one who had negative effects from these practices. I give my advice with care, mindful of the unique individual in front of me, their unique approach to the world, and the fact that some people would run a mile from any suggestion of mindfulness or yoga! One proceeds with caution, care and optimism.

—

Sunday 28 May

Meditation chips along nicely today although I still have much work to do to discipline my mind. Buddha: 'All that we are is the result of what we have thought. The mind is everything.' O dear heavens.

Monday 29 May

Earlier this month (on 2 May, to be precise) I decided that I needed to focus more on the experiential aspect of meditating and reflect more on my contemplative experiences in this journal. I have failed. Throughout May I have continued to write about movies, the cat, my day-to-day life and heaven knows what else. These are all distractions from the task at hand: meditation. I try yet again to focus, but without trying *too* hard, because too much effort is counterproductive. I become deeply, deeply frustrated. This is a familiar feeling.

—

Tuesday 30 May

This morning I am the only person present at the start of my meditation sit. Two other people join me during the sit: one after ten minutes, the other after half an hour.

Before starting, I organise the room, carefully setting out the mats and cushions. I retrieve the 'bell', a handsome bowl that someone strikes gently at the start of the sit, again after thirty minutes and again at the end. This means that the other meditators can simply forget about time until the bell rings again. This is protected space, protected time.

It turns out that the usual bell ringer and room setter-upper is away. I have no watch so the only way I have to keep track of time is with my phone, which I place on silent. I generally do not find it difficult to keep my eyes shut for the hour while I meditate, but today I must keep an eye on my phone from time to time to make sure I ring the bell at the correct moment. This is a small distraction but one's response to such distractions lies at the very heart of meditation. They provide an opportunity mindfully to set one's thoughts aside and focus on one's breathing.

I am especially distracted by my new role today. Being the bell ringer is a serious responsibility. And I *love* it.

Wednesday 31 May

And so another month ends. Where am I with this project? May has been a month of distractions: from Trixie to bell-ringing, from movies to the ceaseless demands of work. The best spin I can possibly put on this is that perhaps this phase is an essential stage in the project: the intensification of distractions as a mandatory component of moving *beyond distraction*, transcending distraction in search of clarity and better meditation practice.

I am not certain that this explanation is true but I am sure that continually berating myself about my apparent failure to progress is unhelpful. I again re-commit to the project and, especially, to sharpening my focus over the coming months.

And then I eat my celebratory end-of-the-month cake. This month it is a plain sponge cake: no icing, no jam, no filling. Just cake. It is left over from some baking at the weekend, when too many sponges were made. It looks a little spartan today, almost Zen. But it is, as ever, delicious.

June

—

In which I meditate as best as possible, try to overcome
frustration, and – in a terrifically unexpected development – actually visit the gym where, arguably, my 'self'
finally dissolves. I contemplate this month's theme from
the noble eightfold path ('right resolve') and reflect on the
relationship between contemplative practice and neuroscience, which is a topic of increasing interest but raises
questions about the purpose of this kind of research: why
do researchers do brain scans on tiny numbers of highly
accomplished meditating monks? What are they trying to
prove? The month also features time spent with the cat,
Trixie, a disquieting domestic catastrophe, a visit from
a lovely dog, Max, a cake sale, quotations from Buddha,
Emerson and the internet, some really splendid ice cream
and (inevitably) more cake. It's an odd mix.

Thursday 1 June

Off we go: another month. More meditation, more random thoughts, more trying to be mindful in day-to-day life. Still, I remain resolutely on course with my meditation project, albeit without any actual spiritual progress, just a sort of gritty determination to keep going.

–

Friday 2 June

Buddha: 'Doubt everything'.

–

Saturday 3 June

I cannot recall a day without frustration. That's *duhkha* for you, I suppose: the ubiquitous, fundamental unsatisfactoriness of everything. Onward, onward. I sit.

–

Sunday 4 June

I visit the gym. I know! Who saw that coming? It's a bank holiday weekend and, after a couple of hours on some research papers, I cycle to the gym at 9.30 am, full of beans. There is hardly anyone here, which is wonderful. Regular gym-goers simply do not understand how off-putting gyms are for people unfamiliar with them: how do the various pieces of equipment work? Am I doing the wrong thing? Do I look silly? What on earth are those people doing over there?

I now understand that a balding, middle-aged man struggling on a treadmill does not attract the attention of the fit young people here. They literally *do not see me*. Perhaps here, in this way, I have finally achieved the 'non-self' of which Buddhism speaks? I am invisible.

Monday 5 June

Lovely bank holiday Monday today. To maintain the momentum from my gym visit yesterday I go for a run in the morning after a couple of hours' work and a fifteen-minute sit. I find some early-morning work settling: drafting articles, revising papers and so on. And a run or a walk is good too, but only when the weather permits. I am a fair-weather runner, a fraud.

But this morning is cool, breezy and quiet on the streets. It is perfect for a contemplative jog, interspersed with periods of walking and just looking around. When I return after around forty-five minutes, Trixie is waiting patiently for me on the doorstep. She knows full well that she can enter the house through her cat flap in the back door any time she wishes, but she often waits to have someone open the front door for her.

–

Tuesday 6 June

Back to work today. I've returned to all the busyness and activity of the workplace so I'm lucky to find a few minutes to sit. I 'just sit' today so as not to become too obsessed with my breathing – a very real form of distraction when one routinely practises the 'mindfulness of breathing'.

I see Tanya again. Tanya continues to self-harm but has started a course of counselling, which is good. She has also decided to cut down and hopefully stop smoking cannabis. She has, unexpectedly, broken up with the partner who suggested she see a psychiatrist in the first place. But progress is often like this: gradual, non-linear and complex. It is also rewarding. Tanya is making real, sustainable progress and she can see that in herself.

–

Wednesday 7 June

I'm on call today. This part of our service is absolutely vital. Mental health problems can reach crisis point at any time and many people find evenings and weekends especially difficult. All major hospitals offer 24-hour emergency psychiatry services, 365 days per year. These are *emergency* services, so one is sometimes a little limited in what one can offer during certain periods (for example at 4 am in a busy emergency department). Nevertheless, psychiatric assessments can and do occur in such settings: people are admitted to psychiatry units for emergency care and others have alternative treatment plans agreed, with follow-up care over subsequent days and weeks.

The situation calms down just before midnight as the flow of patients quietens. But, once again, there will be more tomorrow. And the next day. And the next.

–

Thursday 8 June
This month's theme in my year-long meditation project is 'right resolve', the second element of the noble eightfold path. According to Buddhist literature, right resolve means 'being resolved on renunciation, on freedom from ill will, on harmlessness.' In other words, one must resolve to observe the four noble truths and to live a life informed by the noble eightfold path. That's all a bit circular, surely?

My resolution to meditate every day for a year is probably an example of right resolve; that's to say that without that initial right resolve, my meditation project simply would not have commenced. But I need to renew that right resolve every day and I also need to make other resolutions to support it: resolutions to bring more mindfulness into everyday life, renounce craving and delusion, and care better for all sentient beings – which probably includes, at a minimum, being more considerate towards other people, eating fewer burgers, and being nicer to the cat. (There might be more to it than this, admittedly.)

–

Friday 9 June
Ironically, my right resolve almost falters as I am on call again for the hospital today and tomorrow and things are more than a little pressured. Nonetheless I persevere, consistent with Buddha's advice: 'When faced with the vicissitudes of life, one's mind remains unshaken, sorrow-less, stainless, secure; this is the greatest welfare.' If only.

Saturday 10 June

I spend virtually all of today in the hospital, chiefly seeing people presenting with mental health problems in the emergency department. Appropriately, Buddhism places great emphasis on compassion. It is useful consciously to refocus on compassion every so often throughout a day like today.

In modern mental health care, it is easy to become entirely preoccupied by practicalities. How many people are waiting to be seen? Do we have any empty beds? Are other hospitals operating above capacity and looking for assistance from us? Does this patient have anyone at home if they must go home (or insist on going home) from the emergency department right now, at 3 am?

And – one of the biggest problems – if someone's mental distress is entirely attributable to homelessness, poverty or some other kind of social dysfunction, are there any out-of-hours social services to help them, to avoid an inappropriate 'social admission' to a psychiatry unit? Or is there any other way to avoid discharging them from the emergency department literally onto the street if they don't need inpatient psychiatric care but find themselves destitute for some reason?

Consciously refocusing on compassion from time to time is helpful on a day like today, when one could just end up working furiously with my excellent colleagues for hour after hour after hour, becoming more and more frustrated – frustrated at the stigma and misunderstandings associated with mental illness, frustrated at the inadequacy of Dublin's provision for the homeless mentally ill, frustrated at a criminal justice system that criminalises the mentally ill owing to very minor offending or the simple inability to provide an address and frustrated at the expectation that mental health services are the first port of call for anyone who is violent. The vast majority of mentally ill people are not at all violent and the vast majority of violent people are not mentally ill.

These are all social problems linked with stigma, discrimination and social exclusion of the mentally ill. This situation has to change and the ultimate solutions will be political: persuading politicians to remedy the service deficiencies and injustices experienced by the mentally ill and their families, and persuading government to improve social services for everyone affected by mental illness and psychological problems.

Against this background, consciously refocusing on compassion is sometimes difficult in the acute situation, but it is absolutely essential. It is also a superb way of connecting with people: just sitting with those who present to the emergency department and speaking with genuine compassion and absolute candour. I lose count of how many times I say: 'I don't know the answer here but let's see if we can figure it out.' And: 'You're in a tough spot. We can't solve everything for you now. But let's see what's the best we can do today, and then make a plan for tomorrow.'

Compassion, honesty and absolute straight talking are like magic in this setting, but they are also exhausting. Today wears me out completely but happily my night is disturbed by just a single, brief telephone call at 11 pm. Apart from that I sleep like a log, lost to the world.

—

Sunday 11 June

Bright and blustery today. I'm awake early and work on research papers for three hours. Fifteen minutes of meditation and I'm ready for the world. Today is a much more relaxed affair: reading, hanging around and generally recalibrating after being on call. It is a much-needed kind of day: low energy, low effort, high impact.

—

Monday 12 June

Most spiritual traditions have strong contemplative elements. On the radio last week, I was unexpectedly asked about Sufism, a fascinating and profound form of mystical Islam. There is a Sufi quote: 'Reflection is the lamp of the heart. If it departs, the heart will have no light.' Darkness is not a thing; it is the absence of light.

Tuesday 13 June

Recent decades have seen enormous interest in the neuroscience of Buddhist practice, focused on the central question, What happens to our brains when we meditate? There is now good evidence that sustained meditation produces measurable physical changes to nerve activity and blood flow in certain parts of the brain.

Reflecting on this field of research, I am concerned at how it can be misinterpreted. Linking neuroscience with meditation is not an effort to prove that meditation 'works'. Meditation is an experiential endeavour that does not need the backing of brain scans to prove its worth. This research, rather, seeks to figure out precisely *how* meditation alters brain structure and function, in the same way that scientists study *how* physical exercise alters our muscles, bones and other organs.

Many of these issues are explored by the Mind and Life Institute, an international organisation dedicated to integrating science and contemplative practice, with a deep awareness of social context. Theirs is a reassuringly broad, contextualised endeavour – their website is well worth a look.

–

Wednesday 14 June

Busy day. The cat is in bad form. I sit.

–

Thursday 15 June

This month's book is *Buddhism and Ireland: From the Celts to the Counter-Culture and Beyond* by Laurence Cox. While Buddhism still seems quite exotic to many, it turns out that Ireland and Buddhism have a long history of connection. This is, perhaps, unsurprising given Ireland's notably strong history of contemplative monasticism, chiefly (but not exclusively) linked with Roman Catholicism. It seems that Irish people have encountered Asian Buddhism for over fourteen centuries in many different ways: by travelling to far-off lands, partaking in the more recent secular spread of Buddhist meditation in Ireland and in the form of dedicated spiritual and philosophical studies at individual or group level.

Already this year I have read about U Dhammaloka and Maura O'Halloran. *Buddhism and Ireland* shows how knowledge of Buddhist Asia reached Ireland by the seventh century and the first Irish Buddhists appeared during the political and cultural crisis of the nineteenth century, in Dublin and the rural West, as well as in Burma and Japan. Since the 1960s, Buddhism has expanded to become a relatively common religion in Ireland, although some would argue that Buddhism is not a religion *per se*, but rather a collection of techniques and advice about ways to encounter oneself and the world – techniques and advice that require not blind faith but only belief sufficient to try them in one's life and see how they work out.

–

Friday 16 June

I meditate briefly in the morning and then spend most of the day in my office. I stop briefly to work with some TV documentary-makers looking at the fate of women in Ireland's asylums during the 1900s. There are many sad stories from Ireland's enormous mental hospitals of the 1950s and 1960s, but there are also stories of kindness. Overall, though, this was a troubling period of custody and control in mental healthcare, rather than compassion and care.

Kindness is good; freedom is better.

We must do better.

–

Saturday 17 June

Warm, warm day. I think again about this month's theme, 'right resolve', the second element of the noble eightfold path: 'being resolved on renunciation, on freedom from ill will, on harmlessness'. This is not easy. Most of us are prone to occasional dramatic resolutions, such as New Year's resolutions or decisions to join gyms, which we visit rarely if ever. (I'm somewhere between 'rarely' and 'never' with the gym.)

All resolutions need to be renewed, expanded, developed and adapted to changing circumstances. The best resolutions are dynamic rather than static. I resolve to make fewer, better resolutions, but then get lost in a familiar self-referential haze: is it logical to make a resolution about making fewer, better resolutions? It is better, but it is also more! I resolve to sit and clear my mind, only to realise that this, too, is a resolution. O dear heavens! The Buddhists are right: a clear, settled mind is indeed a treasure beyond all value.

—

Sunday 18 June

Father's Day. I attend a cake sale, visit bookshops and eat pizza. Ice cream also makes an appearance.

I just love the Dublin bookshops: Hodges Figgis, Dubray, Easons, Chapters and all of the other individual outlets scattered across the city. I could spend hours in any of them and I make a particular effort to buy books there. I would be most upset if bookshops vanished from our lives. How else would I stumble across books I would have never otherwise dreamed of reading? I browse in Dubray in Rathmines, utterly contented.

—

Monday 19 June

The weather is so sunny it feels like I should be on holidays but I am not: I am at work.

There are many websites devoted to the relevance of Buddhism in the workplace. Several Buddhist aphorisms, it seems, are intended to apply to work situations:

'Your work is to discover your world and then with all your heart give yourself to it.'

'A lay follower [of Buddha] should not engage in five kinds of business. Which five? Business in weapons, business in human beings, business in meat, business in intoxicants, and business in poison.'

'Good wishes are not enough; we must become actively engaged.'

All good advice, but somewhat vague. And the world of work has undoubtedly changed over the centuries since Buddha wandered the earth. Perhaps the best advice is to try to follow the eightfold path in all places: at home, at work and everywhere in between.

If all goes well with my meditation project, I'll get to consider 'right livelihood' with a little more focus in September. For now I simply carry on working, sitting and doing the million and one other things that make up modern life.

It's all endlessly complicated, sometimes hopelessly so.

–

Tuesday 20 June

We have a high-level domestic catastrophe today. At 7 am the hot water cylinder in the hot press springs a dramatic leak. Consequent events are too painful and disturbing to relate. Did this kind of thing happen to Buddha? Plumbers become involved. This would test anyone's mindfulness. It certainly exceeds mine.

At work I see Deirdre, a twenty-year old university student. Always anxious and shy, Deirdre was a consistent high achiever. Over the course of the past few months, however, Deirdre's family noticed that she was rarely eating at home and was getting steadily thinner. They asked her about this but Deirdre said everything was fine. Some weeks later, however, Deirdre's mother came upon Deirdre making herself vomit in the bathroom. It turns out she was starving herself because she was afraid of being 'fat'. On discussion, Deirdre has a range of other physical and psychological symptoms consistent with an eating disorder such as anorexia nervosa.

As we speak, Deirdre tells me with full sincerity that she fundamentally believes she looks fat. She is dreadfully unhappy. She tells me she wants to change this with a steely determination that impresses me. Eating disorders are treated from the perspectives of both psychological and physical health and are invariably complex. They are among the most challenging conditions to treat but I believe Deirdre will do well. She is clear, confident and well supported. The challenges are great but so too is her resolve. I have profound admiration for the depths of resilience that people often find within themselves at times like this.

I am in simple awe of Deirdre as she sits here in front of me, asking for help.

—

Wednesday 21 June

Book club day! This month we have all read or reread *Bird's Nest Soup* by Hanna Greally, which brings us back to the history of the Irish mental hospitals in the mid 1900s.

Greally was born in Athlone in 1925 and admitted to St Loman's Mental Hospital in Mullingar in 1943, ostensibly for a rest, based on a civil committal signed by her mother, who died six months later. *Bird's Nest Soup* is a thinly veiled, compelling, disturbing account of Greally's nineteen years in St Loman's: grey walls, bad food, lack of privacy, sedatives, liquid paraffin, electroconvulsive and insulin therapy. While some staff members were undoubtedly kind, there were still times when Greally wished she were dead. She tried, on a number of occasions, to escape.

After almost two decades, a change in medical staffing was accompanied by the opening of a new rehabilitation centre to which Greally was discharged in 1962. She went on to work in Ireland and England and wrote poetry, short stories and three full-length manuscripts. *Bird's Nest Soup* appeared in 1971 and Greally made a memorable appearance on *The Late Late Show*. She died in Roscommon in 1987.

We discuss *Bird's Nest Soup* at our book club, which is composed entirely of psychiatrists. There's plenty for us to contemplate in the book, not least the most worrying question of all: are there things that we are doing as psychiatrists today, with the best intentions, that people will look back on with perplexity and disappointment in the future? And how would we know?

We arrange to meet again in September to discuss *The Bell Jar*. I read the novel many years ago and all I remember is that it concerns mental illness. Reading about it online, I learn that Sylvia Plath died by suicide a month after the book's first UK publication in 1963. I order it, along with Plath's collected poems, before going to bed.

–

Thursday 22 June

Mopping up water from the bust hot water cylinder the other day, I fell. I landed on my ribcage – all 70 kg of me straight down onto the left side of my chest. It's still very painful so I have an X-ray today to see if I've broken any ribs. The X-ray looks okay and I'm told that if the pain resolves within a week or two, I didn't break a rib. If the pain lasts for five or six weeks, I probably did break a rib. So we'll see. One must be philosophical, I suppose. The team in the hospital is helpful. Am I that helpful when I'm at work? There's a troubling thought to meditate upon.

–

Friday 23 June

I have a long-standing interest in Ralph Waldo Emerson, the American essayist and poet. While this interest has never really translated into reading much of his work in depth, I am especially struck by this quotation: 'Great men are they who see that spiritual is stronger than any material force – that thoughts rule the world.' I've always meant to read his essay on self-reliance but have never actually done so. I must fix that soon.

Meanwhile, more Emersonian nuggets: 'Do not go where the path may lead, go instead where there is no path and leave a trail.' And: 'To be yourself in a world that is constantly trying to make you something else is the greatest accomplishment.' This is the stuff of posters in teenagers' bedrooms, but much of it is probably true.

It's a soulful, brooding day, with a tinge of melancholy to it.

Saturday 24 June

We watch *20th Century Women* on DVD. I like the movie for its offbeat, reflective tone and its unhurried exploration of the lives of its characters. It is a measured film that slows down frequently and sometimes even pauses, presumably to let the viewer mull over situations that evolve. I like being compelled to slow down. The persisting pain in my ribcage from my fall some days ago has also slowed me down. The pain is regrettable but the slowing down is not. Maybe that is one of the effects of meditation too, to slow us down and make us more mindful?

–

Sunday 25 June

Up early, a couple of hours of work, meditation and then lunch in town, bookshops, some really splendid ice cream, the bus home, a takeaway for tea. We also get a welcome visit from some friends who are collecting a bicycle and bring along their dog Max. Max is almost certainly an enlightened being, living entirely in the moment. It is always a joy to see Max. And, of course, our friends. But also Max.

I know we're only four days past the summer solstice, but I think I see the evenings drawing in. It's probably just my imagination, but there you have it. I haven't even been on summer holiday yet and already I'm feeling autumnal.

I really like Max.

–

Monday 26 June

My ribcage is still sore. Mindfulness can help greatly with pain, especially chronic pain syndromes. There is a great deal of research to support this view and I have seen it work in clinical practice too.

I read an entire book about this once, *Teach Us to Sit Still: A Sceptic's Search for Health and Healing* by Tim Parks. The book centres on the author's chronic pelvic pain and his search for a diagnosis and treatment. After going around the houses for a bit, Parks eventually tries meditation and discovers that while a definitive physical cause cannot be found, his pain isn't nothing: his suffering is real but is simply not adequately explained by current knowledge of biology. Meditation helps Parks in the way that meditation classically does: it seems irrelevant and impossibly hard at first, but for some reason he persists and profound change gradually takes hold. It is quite subtle in the beginning but the transformation is powerful and lasting in the end, which is precisely how meditation tends to operate.

I try this myself today but the pain persists. Perhaps I've broken a rib? I must be patient and philosophical, just like the doctor said. Buddha would agree.

–

Tuesday 27 June

More wisdom from Buddha, courtesy of the internet: 'There is nothing so disobedient as an undisciplined mind, and there is nothing so obedient as a disciplined mind.' This seems obvious, surely? Periods of discipline of mind are indeed remarkable: with good concentration ('right concentration'?), everything is so much easier – and not just a little bit easier, but easier in large, dramatic, different ways that no one can predict.

I also like this quote, which emphasises the importance of individual experience and practice, rather than doctrine, as a foundation for belief:

Do not believe in anything simply because you have heard it. Do not believe in anything simply because it is spoken and rumoured by many. Do not believe in anything simply because it is found written in your religious books. Do not believe in anything merely on the authority of your teachers and elders. Do not believe in traditions because they have been handed down for many generations. But after observation and analysis, when you find that anything agrees with reason and is conducive to the good and benefit of one and all, then accept it and live up to it.

Wednesday 28 June

Busy day at work: barely a moment to sit still. But in the midst of all the hectic activity, I am mindful of this thought, also attributed to Buddha (but who really knows?): 'Every morning we are born again. What we do today is what matters most.'

That is the kind of reincarnation I can believe in: constant renewal and always the possibility of change.

–

Thursday 29 June

For reasons I cannot quite fathom, I'm reading a remarkably popular book called *Hillbilly Elegy*. The author, J.D. Vance, grew up in Middletown, Ohio and Jackson, Kentucky and his memoir focuses on his childhood and background, especially social conditions in Middletown.

Press reports about *Hillbilly Elegy* are nothing short of ecstatic, but I do not like the book. I don't quite know why. The author depicts a certain kind of social dislocation and alienation that I recognise from my clinical work, but although I feel he makes that case very well early on, the remainder of the book is much less compelling. Still, I persist as best I can, mostly because I dislike giving up on books. I'm not certain if this is a good policy or simply a stubborn one.

Grimly, I press on.

–

Friday 30 June

And so I have arrived at the midway point in my year of daily meditation: six months down, six to go. What has changed?

The first thing to strike me is my astonishing lack of spiritual advancement or enlightenment. Despite daily meditation, I'm still ambling along through the world pretty much like I always have. In other words: no dramatic change. Am I more reflective, more mindful, more meditative as a result of my daily sit? I suppose I must be, since I'm meditating for fifteen minutes per day. But what about the other 1,425 minutes in each day; am I any different during those? Probably not, although I do remain marginally more aware of my passing mental states than before, which is good.

And while I might not have levitated or achieved enlightenment, there is still much to note on the positive side of the balance sheet. To my great surprise I've proven dedicated to this project: I greatly enjoy the meditation itself (especially when I make it to the meditation centre for the silent, early morning sits); and I have, finally, for the first time in my life, managed to keep a journal. Also, I am told that the reason why Max, our friend's dog, likes me is because I am calm and Max likes calmness. Surely that means something?

I can't really see anything to put on the negative side of the balance sheet. My work and home lives have not missed the fifteen minutes that I spend meditating each day: it's not as if my work or home lives were ever so rigorously timetabled that they would suffer because I set aside a quarter of an hour for daily meditation. But I must acknowledge some disappointment that I haven't motivated myself to spend longer periods meditating, especially in the past month or two; that I haven't made greater effort to go to the early-morning meditation sits more frequently; that I haven't gone on a meditation retreat; and that my meditation has not become more profound.

But there's no point being hard on myself. I take these points on board in the spirit of right resolve.

And then I eat my end-of-month cake which is, as ever, delicious. This month it's chocolate biscuit cake, which isn't really cake at all, but broken biscuits embedded in a wonderful slab of chocolate. This was always my chosen birthday cake as a child and I remain very fond of it. The addition of marshmallows, making it into 'rocky road', has never impressed me in the slightest. Today I stick with old-style chocolate biscuit cake to mark the end of six months of my meditation project.

I love cake.

And Max.

I really love Max.

July

—

RIGHT SPEECH

In which I reflect on Zen Buddhism, Thoreau in the wilderness and the mysterious wanderings of Trixie. This month's theme, 'right speech', puzzles as much as it enlightens, and I touch down in Prague where I see a man in a tea shop who is (I hope) the future me. I am compelled to reflect – not for the first time – on self-immolation, which is when a person deliberately burns himself or herself, generally as a form of political protest and often with fatal consequences. It is a confusing feature of Buddhist history. My summer travels bring me to Berlin for the first time and I love it. Throughout my meanderings, I am forced to confront the disturbing fact that, half a year through my year of meditation, I am still meditating very poorly indeed. As a result, it looks like my journal will turn out to be about a year spent meditating badly rather than a year spent meditating well. Does it matter? Yes, it almost certainly does. Other themes come and go throughout the month: the effects of meditation on the brain, the importance of acceptance, Greek philosophy, tranquillity of mind and a million other disparate, distracting thoughts.

Saturday 1 July

And so I start into another month. It also feels like the beginning of summer (which, in fairness, it is). My sit is continually interrupted by thoughts of how I should be sitting longer, doing better and generally being an improved meditator. It is difficult to shake such thoughts from my mind. Repeatedly I try and repeatedly I fail. Am I getting any better at this? How would I know if I was improving? Perhaps I'll never know.

There is a Zen saying: 'Before enlightenment, chop wood, carry water. After enlightenment, chop wood, carry water.'

Enlightenment is a common but difficult-to-understand concept in Buddhism: it is presented as the ultimate goal of spiritual practice but one must not crave enlightenment because that would be un-Buddhist. For me, enlightenment remains so far distant that this is not an issue I need to navigate any time soon. Today I just sit.

–

Sunday 2 July

Another Zen saying: 'To study the way of the Buddha is to study oneself. To study oneself is to forget oneself. To forget oneself is to be enlightened by everything.'

–

Monday 3 July

This month's theme in my year-long meditation project is 'right speech', the third element of the noble eightfold path. Buddhist literature asks: 'And what is right speech? Abstaining from lying, from divisive speech, from abusive speech, and from idle chatter: This is called right speech.' I think 'idle chatter' is the big risk here.

–

Tuesday 4 July

More guidance on right speech: 'Monks, a statement endowed with five factors is well-spoken, not ill-spoken. It is blameless and unfaulted by knowledgeable people. Which five? It is spoken at the right time. It is spoken in truth. It is spoken affectionately. It is spoken beneficially. It is spoken with a mind of good-will.'

In this context, it is interesting that the noble eightfold path did not also include 'right silence'. I can think of many occasions in my life when right silence would have served me well. Perhaps now is one of those occasions?

I start reading Jon Krakauer's *Into the Wild*, which recounts the young narrator Chris McCandless's travels across the US and beyond and his eventual trip to Alaska, where he entered the wilderness in a woefully unprepared state. It is a tragic tale. McCandless was influenced by *Walden, or Life in the Woods*, Thoreau's classic transcendentalist text. Thoreau proposed living a simple life in natural surroundings. McCandless played the same game but at a much higher level of risk and he paid the ultimate price. His story is interesting but I cannot identify with him in the slightest: I have never felt his need to renounce civilisation to anything like that extent.

But there is an interesting Buddhist parallel here. According to traditional sources, Buddha renounced his life of privilege and went in search of enlightenment, leaving his wife and child behind – but Buddha was searching for enlightenment within himself, whereas McCandless believed he had already found enlightenment in raw nature. There is a difference. And there is nothing enlightened about being dead.

–

Wednesday 5 July

I'm still thinking about *Into the Wild* and Thoreau. Thoreau's life and philosophy were far more Buddhist than those of McCandless. Thoreau advocated what we now know as 'mindfulness': 'You must live in the present, launch yourself on every wave, find your eternity in each moment.' And: 'Wealth is the ability to fully experience life.' And: 'Live your beliefs and you can turn the world around.' And why did Thoreau famously choose a life in the woods, away from civilisation?

'I went to the woods because I wished to live deliberately, to front only the essential facts of life, and see if I could not learn what it had to teach, and not, when I came to die, discover that I had not lived.' But Thoreau, in common with all good Buddhist teachers, warns against blind dogmatism: 'I left the woods for as good a reason as I went there. Perhaps it seemed to me that I had several more lives to live and could not spare any more time for that one.'

It's all very mindful. I like Thoreau.

—

Thursday 6 July

Each morning, when I get up and go downstairs, Trixie is waiting for me in the kitchen. She is always keen to go outside but she is also aware that I am a good source of treats (specifically cheese). I open the cat flap but Trixie, torn between conflicting desires to rush outside or to await treats inside, rubs around my legs for a little while in the hope of some cheese. At a certain point, if she decides that cheese is not forthcoming, she will exit through the cat flap, climb over the back wall, and vanish. I have no idea where she goes. Only Trixie knows.

This 'not knowing' is important to me. I have always liked that Trixie has her secrets, that she has a life of her own that is unknowable to me. Over the course of this meditation project, however, I've come to realise just how much I like this unknowability. I like it a great deal, it turns out.

My days are mostly filled with purposive thoughts, cognitive challenges, cluttered timetables and deliberate actions with relatively predictable consequences. Like much modern life, my day is over-determined, entirely charted out in advance. Trixie's secrets are a glorious counterpoint to this, true mysteries in a world increasingly devoid of them. Meditation has helped me appreciate this more and more, and to place greater value on things that I do not know, that I cannot know, and that literally cannot be known. These vacuums are like sacred spaces in a world that is over-scheduled and over-literal.

Meditating on the mysterious and sitting with the unknowable are, perhaps, the greatest gifts. Trixie helps with both.

Friday 7 July

I'm thinking about 'right speech' today, this month's theme. It is difficult *always* to abstain from 'idle chatter', *always* to speak 'at the right time', 'in truth', 'affectionately', 'beneficially' and 'with a mind of good-will.' In fact, it's impossible. But still, I suppose one must try. The greatest difficulty lies with people who are, in my eyes, being unreasonable.

There is a concept called the 'fundamental attribution error', which is a tendency to over-attribute other people's unreasonable behaviour to their character and under-attribute it to their circumstances or situation. In other words, if someone else is unreasonable, I conclude that he or she is an unreasonable person. If I am unreasonable, I tell myself it's because I'm under pressure, or busy, or in exceptional circumstances that somehow excuse my behaviour. We are less forgiving when judging others. For me, I conclude that unreasonableness is due to circumstances; for others, it's their personalities.

This useful concept strongly supports the importance of right speech. One must avoid reflex harsh words against others: they might be under pressure in ways we don't understand.

Of course, this is all very well in theory but difficult in practice.

And it is virtually impossible in rush-hour traffic.

–

Saturday 8 July

Prague! I'm here for a week-long meeting about mental health and the law. Mental health law and protecting the human rights of the mentally ill are key themes in my work so this is an important meeting for me.

And it's taking place in Prague! I visited Prague only once before, around twenty years ago. I loved it then. And, arriving late tonight, I see the old town in darkness, with the castle across the river, and memories come flooding back. I remember especially the Reduta Jazz Club and our visit to the castle. While we were looking around the castle a large group of male German tourists suddenly began to sing: booming, enthusiastic and really quite excellent. Apparently they were a choir on tour across Europe and their utterly unexpected song was a wonderful unscripted moment at the castle.

Sunday 9 July

Ambling along Wenceslas Square after the conference today we spot a sign for a Nepalese tea shop down a small alleyway. At the end of the lane we find a lovely tea shop selling thousands of different kinds of tea, Nepalese wooden products, books about Buddhism and similar items. It's all very atmospheric and pleasant.

At one table, a bearded, hippy-ish man in his sixties is a picture of calm absorption: working steadily at his laptop, happily engrossed in his writing, a bowl of green tea set on the table in front of him. His big grey beard is particularly fine and a little wild. Will I be like him in the future, when I'm in my sixties? Still typing contentedly into this journal or another one? Or something else entirely? Hopefully I will be just like him, except, perhaps, for the beard. I'm a bit puzzled by the recent trend for complex, manicured facial hair, although, in fairness, this man's beard is not exactly manicured. It's a bit feral.

I could do a lot worse than turn out like this free-spirited man in twenty years' time, working on my laptop down an alleyway in Prague, enjoying Nepalese tea.

–

Monday 10 July

Early each morning, just after 7 am, drilling starts somewhere near my hotel in Prague city centre. The drilling is not too loud, just a background drone. I am always awake well before it starts, but the drilling is quite relentless and can be distracting. As a result, a period of the day that should be excellent for meditation – early morning, in a hotel room, far from home – is imperfect. This is, of course, no surprise: *duhkha* is ubiquitous. I try to respond exactly as meditation teachers suggest: observing the drilling as a distraction, not engaging with it, letting it drift past, focusing on my breath. I do not succeed. But my lack of success has many roots and the drilling is possibly the least of them. I press on.

Tuesday 11 July

On 16 January 1969 a twenty-year-old Czech student named Jan Palach self-immolated to protest against the end of the Prague Spring. Palach died of his burns in a Prague hospital three days later.

I am deeply interested in self-immolation given its association with Buddhism, most recently seen in the wave of self-immolation of Tibetan Buddhist monks and nuns protesting against Chinese domination of Tibet. Such actions bear, at best, an uneasy relationship with Buddhist respect for life.

This evening, after the conference ends for the day, we visit the memorial to Jan Palach and Jan Zajíc, another Czech student who self-immolated in 1969 in front of the National Museum in Wenceslas Square, just up from our hotel. The small memorial is near a busy street in front of a popular museum. It is indescribably sad to think of these young people feeling so voiceless that the only or best form of protest they felt open to them was burning themselves to death.

–

Wednesday 12 July

I was at the conference all day, had a short walk around Prague in the evening and spent fifteen minutes meditating somewhere in the middle. It's an excellent conference: I'm learning lots and enjoying Prague. We attended an especially memorable concert by the Czech National Symphony Orchestra in the gorgeous Rudolfinum concert hall on the banks of the Vltava River.

–

Thursday 13 July

I love to visit bookshops in other countries. After the conference, we visit the Palác knih Luxor (the Neoluxor Palace of Books) on Wenceslas Square. It is an enormous place where I could happily spend many hours. Most of the books are in Czech but that is part of the joy: I see which Czech titles I can identify as translations of popular books in English; I note the sizes of the thematic sections of the shop compared to Irish bookshops (more politics, less fiction); and I investigate the English-language selection (extensive and excellent). I especially like seeing European editions of books that I've read or am interested in buying. The European editions often look and feel different, which is oddly interesting.

I have always been particularly impressed by bookshops in France too, especially their shelves and shelves of Gallimard editions. Many French bookshops convey a reverence for books that is rarely found elsewhere, although there is more than a hint of it here in Prague. Also, the soul-destroying crush of books about diet and cooking is not as oppressive here as it is in Ireland, which is a substantial relief.

–

Friday 14 July

The meeting in Prague ended this afternoon and was most informative. It was a meeting of the International Academy of Law and Mental Health, focused on the role of law in relation to the treatment of mental illness. This focus is very necessary: people with mental illness suffer disproportionate violations of rights ranging from loss of liberty to difficulties accessing care, from increased rates of homelessness to increased risk of imprisonment. The latter is especially disturbing: prisons are toxic for the mentally ill.

These are topics I've been researching, writing and talking about for many years, but I never cease to be disturbed by how great the injustices are. The World Health Organisation points out that 14 per cent of the global burden of disease is attributed to mental, neurological and substance-use disorders, but that most of the people affected – up to 75 per cent in some low-income countries – do not have access to the treatment they need. Tragically, this injustice can be measured not just in terms of access to services but also in outcomes: men with schizophrenia die 15 years earlier, and women 12 years earlier, than the rest of the population. This excess is not accounted for by unnatural deaths; the leading causes are heart disease and cancer. As a result there is a need for enhanced focus on both the mental and physical health of the mentally ill, including extra support in stopping smoking, improved diet and lifestyle and screening for cardiac risk factors. Treatment with antipsychotic medication also significantly reduces the likelihood of premature death in schizophrenia.

The injustices experienced by the mentally ill are fixable. This meeting is a good opportunity to discuss ways to use law to achieve this goal and improve the lives of the mentally ill and their families.

Meditation also helps in situations of injustice like this. Anger is not enough. In fact, anger is counterproductive and unhelpful. Meditation, on the other hand, does not suggest that we accept injustice but rather that we acknowledge it calmly, sit with it, start by changing ourselves, and then move on to change the world in incremental, sustainable ways.

As a result, meditation has helped me not so much accept these dreadful statistics about global mental health (they are utterly unacceptable), but rather to examine them with care, see how I can try to help in my day-to-day life and work, and then see how matters might be improved more broadly.

These are big tasks that need to be undertaken calmly and in small steps. Meditation makes this clearer.

–

Saturday 15 July

We leave Prague today. One of the unexpected, last-minute highlights of our trip is a visit to the 'Art of Asia' exhibition at the National Gallery, housed in the Kinský Palace on the Old Town Square. They have a lovely collection of paintings, wall hangings, artefacts and figures of Buddha. Afterwards, in a neighbouring shop, I buy a wonderful seated Buddha. My collection is growing. If only I could spend more time meditating and less time buying Buddhas!

We also enjoy a visit to the Convent of St Agnes of Bohemia, now a lovingly restored part of the National Gallery in Prague: moody, atmospheric, settling.

Prague is an amazing place. I have a real fondness for great European cities: Amsterdam, Madrid, Paris, Prague, Copenhagen and Rome, as well as my three all-time favourites: Stockholm, Budapest and St Petersburg. We are sad to leave Prague but nonetheless head stoically to the airport, braced for the ritual indignities of cheap air travel. Budget airlines present a real test of mindfulness; I reflect on this further in an essay at the end of this month.

–

Sunday 16 July

I am on my own in Dublin for the next few days and take full advantage of my situation and head to the cinema to see *Sanctuary*. I enjoy the film hugely although its ultimate message is a sad one: that we have yet to offer people with intellectual disabilities meaningful opportunities for full participation in society.

Afterwards I cross from the Irish Film Institute on Eustace Street to another regular haunt, Monty's of Kathmandu, for the usual: chicken choila and chicken chilli nanglo (both extra hot) with jasmine rice. No words can explain how much I enjoy this. Try it and see.

–

Monday 17 July

For this month's book I'm looking at *Zen-Brain Reflections: Reviewing Recent Developments in Meditation and States of Consciousness* by James H. Austin. During a sabbatical in Kyoto, Austin began Zen meditation training with Kobori-Roshi, a Rinzai Zen master, and has now completed several decades of brain research involving neurology, neuropathology, neuro-chemistry and contemplative neuroscience. I previously enjoyed one of Austin's earlier books on similar themes, *Zen and the Brain: Towards an Understanding of Meditation and Consciousness*.

Both books centre on Austin's explorations of interrelationships between Zen Buddhism and brain research. What most attracts me to Austin's work is his integration of neuroscience with his own personal experiences. He also looks at areas such as the placebo effect and acupuncture, neuroimaging and changes in physiology associated with meditation, as well as various states of absorption – and even the possible links between migraines and metaphors, moonlight and mysticism, and all kinds of other themes.

It is, perhaps, the expansiveness of Austin's vision that impresses most, his coupling of painstaking study and attention to detail with a willingness to look at the big, big concepts in meditation. It's hard not to be impressed by his striving to chart a pathway through it all, centred firmly on understanding, meaning and enlightenment. I enjoy revisiting his writing, looking around his website and reflecting on his work. Of course, all of this has new relevance for me now, as I try to integrate meditation with my daily life and think about the links between meditation and my work, often through this diary. There is much to reflect upon.

–

Tuesday 18 July

I have never smoked a cigarette in my life but I sometimes envy smokers. This evening I see a young woman smoking outside a hotel, standing on her own by the entrance and gazing into the middle distance. The need to smoke has brought her into a solitary and potentially contemplative space in which she takes time away from the events of the day and just smokes. While smoking is basically a slow-burn form of self-harm and there is absolutely nothing enlightened about it, I sometimes envy that space that smokers create as they step away from the crowd to fulfil their habit. The trick is to be able to do that without the cigarette, I suppose.

Inevitably, a quick online search reveals a great deal of discussion about smoking and meditation, with stories, anecdotes and advice aplenty. There are even smoking cessation techniques based on mindfulness, which seems like a good idea: the act of smoking, especially solitary smoking, is surely one that lends itself to mindfulness, which can then be used as a pathway to cessation.

Still, having never smoked a cigarette (or anything else for that matter), I am scarcely in a position to give anyone advice about this. So I'll stop.

In the clinic I see Greg, a 65-year old man who drinks two bottles of whiskey a day. He lives alone in a damp, decaying house. There are rats. He comes to see me today solely in order to keep his son happy. Greg is unkempt and poorly dressed but expresses no desire to stop drinking despite its adverse effects on his physical and mental health. Greg tells me he understands that alcohol is killing him and I think he does understand this. But it is hard to know if his decision-making capacity is impaired owing to decades of alcohol abuse. Does he have the mental capacity to decide about this? I find his case troubling. At what point should someone intervene in this situation?

We talk for almost an hour. Eventually Greg agrees to see me again in a month's time and to let the public health nurse visit in the meantime. That's something. Supporting someone to change a long-standing habit like Greg's drinking can be very, very difficult. I hope it's not too late here – but, of course, it's never too late.

–

Wednesday 19 July
The movie I saw last Sunday, *Sanctuary*, is still playing on my mind, possibly because it is so rare to see people with intellectual disabilities in feature films. Ireland's historical treatment of people with intellectual disabilities has been quite varied. The part of that history that I know best concerns the institutionalisation of the intellectually disabled in the large asylums and mental hospitals of the 1800s and 1900s. In 1907 Dr Conolly Norman, the progressive, outspoken medical superintendent at the Richmond District Asylum (later St Brendan's Hospital, Dublin, now part of Technological University Dublin), lamented the absence of proper services for people with intellectual disability: 'It is neither wise nor humane to neglect this class as they are neglected in this country.'

Thursday 20 July

Aristotle reportedly said that 'it is the mark of an educated mind to be able to entertain a thought without accepting it'. This is akin to mindfulness: observing a thought but not becoming engaged with it; noting the thought's presence but letting it drift past. More thoughts will come and they too can drift past. This is a key skill of meditation. And meditation is, in Buddhist thought, central to spiritual progress. Aristotle again: 'The energy of the mind is the essence of life.' Meditation is the energy and essence of Buddhism.

–

Friday 21 July

Numerous websites recommend keeping a meditation journal as you start or restart meditating, but I don't think that the kind of journal I am now writing (and you are now reading) is what they have in mind. In its defence, this journal is an honest reflection of the way my mind hops from topic to topic, from meditation to movies, from work to holidays, from random musings to the internet. Focus is difficult; that's why we meditate.

Even so, I should probably concentrate a little more on the actual meditation and provide more detailed accounts of what I'm doing, if this diary is truly to be a meditation journal. But let's face it: this simply has not happened to date. Moreover, I cannot exclude the context within which I'm trying to meditate, especially because the purpose of meditation is not to have a perfect meditation sit, but to improve your life at other times, when you are not meditating.

Even so, a little more focus wouldn't do any harm.

–

Saturday 22 July

Galway! I'm now on two weeks' leave and the sun is shining here in Galway. The streets are full of visitors, the river glistens in the sunlight and the whole place is bursting with energy. What could be better? I must try to meditate more but I must not try *too* hard. It's a difficult balance. I sit in the sun and think about it for some time. Then I just sit in the sun.

Sunday 23 July

Yesterday we saw *Baby Driver*, an action film that makes no attempt at realism: this is definitely for the best in a movie of this type, based almost entirely on fast cars, shooting and thrills. There is precious little by way of mindfulness. By way of contrast, today we see an Australian circus show called *Driftwood* in the Galway International Arts Festival, a glorious, balletic acrobatic display, combining extraordinary athleticism with extraordinary grace. The performers are perfectly in tune with each other, relying completely on their teamwork as they lift each other up, dive into each other's arms, and coordinate their moves with unbelievable shared understanding. They have clearly developed a level of mutual understanding that transcends language and cognition, rooted in physicality, relationships and trust. This is not precisely what meditation seeks to do but neither is it a million miles away from it. Both this kind of performance and meditation seek to encounter the world in a direct, unmediated way, and so to better know reality. It is inspiring stuff.

–

Monday 24 July

Zhuangzi, a Chinese philosopher in the fourth century BC: 'Flow with whatever may happen and let your mind be free. Stay centred by accepting whatever you are doing. This is the ultimate.' Right now, I am writing in this journal, so this is 'the ultimate' right now, yes? It sounds a little dramatic.

–

Tuesday 25 July

We fly to Berlin for a week's holiday. I've never been here before, despite my happy weakness for European cities. We reach our apartment on a busy city street at nightfall and a rabbit is sitting outside the door.

It scampers away as we approach. The mysterious life of the Berlin rabbit reminds me of the unknowable life of Trixie the Dublin cat. As I've meditated over the past few months, I have come to appreciate mysteries far more than I do their solutions. Sitting with not knowing is the essence of meditation.

–

Wednesday 26 July

It is a wet day in Berlin but we visit some shops and the Jewish Museum, which provides a fascinating, disturbing account of German-Jewish history over two millennia. Plenty to meditate about here.

–

Thursday, 27 July

Berlin Zoo! Pandas!

The inner lives of pandas are a mystery to me and, I imagine, to everyone. But the Berlin pandas are a delight and they distract me a little from my meditation today. As ever, I try to let the images of pandas drift out of my mind in the Berlin apartment and focus on my breath. It works. Meditation is often better when I'm on a trip, possibly owing to fewer of my habitual distractions being around.

I dream about pandas; they really are incredibly cute.

–

Friday 28 July

It is time, I think, to confront a cold, hard fact about my meditation project. I am more than halfway through my year of daily meditation and I am still not meditating especially well, most days. As a result, it looks ever more certain that my project will turn out to be about a year spent meditating badly rather than a year spent meditating well. Does it matter? I wish I could say it does not (all effort is good effort, etc.) but it probably does matter. Surely I need at least some progress to report rather than simply carrying on just because I started?

I resolve to try harder (right resolve?) but I also resolve not to crave for progress because that would be unskilful. It's definitely a tricky balance but, even so, I'm fairly certain that I should be doing better than I am at this stage. I settle on an attitude of self-compassion for the day but a part of me still berates myself for my failure to meditate better and more.

Googling Confucius gives me some comfort: 'It does not matter how slowly you go, as long as you do not stop.'

–

Saturday 29 July

More Confucius: 'Life is really simple, but we insist on making it complicated.' But day-to-day life *is* complicated in certain ways and there's no point denying it. We just need to ignore unnecessary complexities. Skilful meditation helps: 'The more man meditates upon good thoughts, the better will be his world and the world at large.'

–

Sunday 30 July

Berlin is a lovely city, busy, exciting, full of history. The streets present a curious mixture of old and new. There are reminders of the Berlin Wall everywhere: sometimes direct remnants of the wall itself, sometimes celebrations of its absence. Both kinds of remembrance matter.

In many ways, the structure and architecture of the city have evolved to reflect its tumultuous past. Berlin does not try to hide its wall or its history, but rather sits with them, as in meditation: seeing reality as it really is. It is as if the city itself physically articulates the complexity of its past, the decisions and actions that changed the history of Europe and the world, and the horrors of the twentieth-century wars. The city does not try to hide these things, does not try to over-interpret them and does not try to somehow make uncomfortable facts disappear. The city sits with the plain, unvarnished truths and building blocks of the past. It is an essentially meditative endeavour and one that Berlin does very well.

Monday 31 July

And so another month ends. As with previous months, I have sustained a modest daily meditation habit but have failed to progress in terms of either spending more time meditating or achieving greater depth. It is exceptionally difficult to know if I am persisting with this project owing to simple stubbornness or to genuine meditative engagement. I also feel a peculiar pressure to continue meditating because I committed to keeping this journal. Even though no one is reading it as I write, the journal still exerts considerable pressure on me to persist.

Once again today, at month's end, I resolve to meditate more and better, and to engage with my project with more heartfelt dedication rather than routine box-ticking. I must, however, retain an element of habit: habit is a strong force in life and the first step in any long-term meditative commitment is to make meditation into a daily habit.

So it is time to acknowledge that meditation is now a daily habit; recognise that it is time to move on to better meditation practices; exercise some self-compassion about my failure to do this over the past few months; and then eat some delicious and (I hope) well-earned end-of-month cake. This month, I reach for a rather substantial wedge of pear and almond frangipane, an incredibly fancy cake from an incredibly fancy bakery here in Berlin. To be honest, I could take or leave the pears but I have a fatal weakness for almonds. And today, in Berlin, this is a fitting end to another month of daily meditation.

» Fly like Buddha: A Practical Guide for the Spiritual Tourist

Travel is exciting but the experience of travelling can be incredibly stressful. Modern air travel can be particularly frustrating, especially on low-cost airlines. Common negative effects include extraordinary irritation, increased emotionality, anxiety and jet-lag. Fifteen per cent of men are more likely to cry at a movie on an airplane than at home. The altered oxygen levels in airplane cabins also affect memory and concentration, making air travel significantly more stressful than any of us would wish.

I have often wondered if lessons from mindfulness, meditation and Buddhism could help with some of these problems. Help us cope better in the air. What follows is a guide to addressing some of these travel challenges, combining traditional medical advice with additional psychological techniques to help get through airports and flights without too much psychological damage.

In order to minimise the negative effects of travel, there is much psychological sense in the usual travel advice: plan trips with care, especially when travelling with children; spend extra money and time if they ease transitions in the journey (leaving plenty of time for meals, rest and connections); bring twice as much money as you think you need, and half as much luggage.

If you are flying, mentally prepare yourself for the inevitable psychological turbulence of modern air travel. Mindfulness and acceptance help greatly. This means accepting a certain loss of control both at airports and in the air. Accept the facts that you will queue up many times at the airport, the queues will be unfair and people will get away with boorish, unsocial behaviour. This is inevitable. You cannot change it; you do not run the airport and you cannot redesign human nature.

If there are more than two lines at check-in or security, you are statistically unlikely to be in the fastest one. If there are 10 lines, there's just a 10 per cent chance that you're in the fastest one and a 90 per cent chance that you're not. Yet we feel annoyed if any one line is faster than ours. Do not fight this apparent injustice. Accept it. Changing lines is futile: if there are more than two lines, you're statistically unlikely to switch to the fastest one. You can't beat the numbers on this (or on anything). Breathe.

Proceed mindfully through the airport. Do not wear headphones during transitions from your car to the check-in area, security to shopping, boarding area to airplane. Move with awareness and connection: this is a journey, not a dream, so stay connected with your surroundings.

The usual travel advice is to stay well hydrated and visit the bathroom whenever you can. This advice applies when travelling by foot, bicycle, car, bus, train, camel or hot air balloon, but needs adjustment for airports, which are basically vast networks of bathrooms joined together by shops and runways. So, when in airports, be sure to stay well hydrated but maybe only visit the bathroom on arrival at the airport, in response to interim need (see how it goes), and immediately prior to boarding. (This advice does not apply to Ranchi airport in northern India where you should use any bathroom you can find and be deeply thankful that you found one at all.)

At the boarding gate, do not stand in line waiting to board the airplane. Stay seated in the boarding area until most people have boarded. The positives of this strategy (sitting down, quietude, control) greatly exceed the negatives (standing up, possibly having your cabin baggage placed in the hold).

On the airplane, take time to settle into your seat, organise your reading or listening material with care and pack away your belongings tidily.

Relax. Your logical brain knows that travelling by airplane is overwhelmingly safer than travelling by car. Your emotional side might not respond to this logic but it will respond to a calm mind and a settled physical demeanour. We make ourselves anxious by acting anxious. Again, breathe.

If you get especially anxious while flying, listening to mindless music is an excellent idea. The perfect airplane song is probably 'Ooh Ooh Baby' from Britney Spears's justly neglected 2007 album *Blackout*. The chorus is especially undemanding: the word 'baby' is repeated 23 times. Compared to this, Taylor Swift's lyrics are Dostoyevskian. 'Teeth' by Lady Gaga is a new contender for best mindless airplane song ever, but I still think Britney shades it.

In the event of turbulence, sit calmly with both feet planted firmly on the floor, hands on your knees, head upright. Remove your headphones, put away your book and focus on your breath. Use the experience as an exercise in yielding control. Acknowledge and embrace the powerlessness: it is paradoxically liberating. Like all forms of liberty, it can be scary. But while you cannot control the turbulence in the slightest, you can control your reaction to it. Reflect explicitly on your lack of agency and simply abide. Link your anxiety with the turbulence and then feel both pass, like an unwanted thought in meditation or an unwanted emotion in life. They all pass.

When the airplane lands, stand up immediately *only* if you desperately need to stretch your legs. Otherwise, there is *absolutely no point* spending 20 minutes standing in a weird, cramped position waiting to 'de-plane'. You will just become restless and agitated while everyone takes their bags down, doubles back for their coats and organises their children off the plane. Stand up only when you can disembark. Again, the positives of this strategy (sitting down, quietude, control) greatly exceed the negatives (standing up, agitating yourself, getting irritated).

Once off the airplane, visit the first bathroom you encounter, or possibly the second if the queue is too long in the first. Never wait for the third: it is being cleaned.

Finally, stay calm, fly like Buddha and remember to enjoy your flight. You'll do it all again on the way home.

August

—

RIGHT ACTION

In which another month begins and again I am determined to stick grittily (if not gracefully) with my fifteen
minutes of daily meditation. Even so, my path is
non-linear, meandering. This month, my journal touches
on Berlin (again), Wexford, the joy of 'being found' and
this month's theme in my year-long meditation project,
'right action', which incorporates Buddhism's strong
prohibition on killing. There are also reflections on
Sufism ('mystical Islam'), Buddhism's 'five hindrances'
to meditation, tranquillity of mind (elusive), distraction (ubiquitous) and my lack of meditative progress
(an inevitable, recurring theme). In what is for me a big
step, I extend my daily meditation from fifteen minutes
to twenty. Bats, foxes, lobsters, past lives, ghosts and
Buddhist poets all feature. Trixie puzzles and delights as
she sits, Sphinx-like, watching my clumsy progress with
quiet, contemplative bemusement.

Tuesday 1 August

I start the new month on the final day of our week-long holiday in Berlin. In the morning we have arranged to visit the Reichstag. I love parliament buildings and this is an especially impressive one. The Reichstag has a magnificent dome with views across the city.

The last day of any holiday is always sad but we had a good stay here. The trip has also given me plenty of food for thought. Perhaps the most poignant moment was a visit to a memorial to the victims of 'Aktion T4', a programme of 'involuntary euthanasia' of over 70,000 people at extermination centres located in psychiatric hospitals in Germany, Austria and Poland. As a psychiatrist, to me this was one of the most profoundly disturbing features of Nazi Germany, resulting in the deliberate, cold-blooded deaths of so many mentally ill and intellectually disabled people. The memorial to them in Berlin is both understated and overwhelming.

–

Wednesday 2 August

We are back in Ireland today but I am not back to work for another week! We are spending the remainder of our time off around Ireland. I like travelling, despite my chronic problems with sleep in different locations. The internet commonly attributes to Buddha the aphorism that 'it is better to travel well than to arrive'. It is also attributed to any number of other people. Whatever its origin, there is much truth in it.

But even if 'it is better to travel well than to arrive', there is still great joy in arriving. This is linked to a concept I once heard a seven-year-old girl express during a game of hide-and-seek. She always hid in plain sight and was found immediately. When I asked why she didn't hide properly she responded, 'I like being found.'

Thursday 3 August

I wake up in Wexford. We came here yesterday to stay for five days in a lovely apartment on the quayside. I go for an early-morning walk on a sunny pier and meet a ladybird, also on a morning walk. The ladybird seems intent on getting to the other side of the pier and scuttles away purposefully.

I sit and meditate unobtrusively for fifteen minutes. Meditation outside is quite different from inside. Happily, the quay is quiet at this early hour but there are still distractions: the wind, birds, occasional cars. These all make me mindful of the present moment but I'm also keen to unhitch from passing sounds and focus on my breath. In the end I have only a small degree of success with the meditation, but I have a refreshing spell outside.

–

Friday 4 August

This month's theme in my year-long meditation project is 'right action', the fourth element in the noble eightfold path. Buddhist literature provides rather direct advice about this month's theme: 'And what is right action? Abstaining from killing, abstaining from stealing, abstaining from sexual misconduct. This is called right action.'

The Buddhist prohibition on killing is very strong, extending to all sentient beings: humans, animals, birds, insects and, some would say, plants. Most Buddhists, however, do not regard plants as sentient. Even so, most suggest avoiding unnecessary harm to plants or other aspects of our natural environment.

All of these prohibitions do not appear especially challenging at first because most people abhor cruelty to humans or animals, and while many people kill insects from time to time, most try to avoid it. And few people set out deliberately to harm plants: Buddhism is strongly consistent with environmental consciousness.

The Buddhist prohibition on killing becomes rather more challenging in relation to food because it points firmly to vegetarianism. I fail deeply here because, as this journal repeatedly demonstrates, burgers and other forms of meat are a key feature of my life. As a result, any progress I make in relation to this month's element of the eightfold path will be incremental: more vegetables, less meat and, hopefully, only the occasional burger.

–

Saturday 5 August

We need to talk about the cat. Trixie has been dispatched to a cattery for almost a month while we have work done on the house. It is a nice cattery but it is still a cattery. We phone to see how she is getting on and the man there says she is doing fine. This may well be the case but Trixie is at her happiest when she is at home in our house, prowling around the back garden or curled up on someone's lap. I hope she will settle back into the house when she returns. It will take her some time to adjust to new floors, repainted walls etc., but cats are pretty adaptable, I'm told. I am considerably less so and I worry about her.

–

Sunday 6 August

I have a weakness for newspapers – old-fashioned, printed newspapers. Every Saturday I buy *The Irish Times, The Guardian* and *The Financial Times*. I even buy *The New York Times International Edition* on occasion, especially when I'm on holiday (as I am now, in Wexford).

In one of these newspapers I read a feature about places in Ireland that offer facilities for solitary contemplative retreats, where you stay in or near a monastery or contemplative centre for a few days, participate (or not) in their programmes and classes and have opportunity for as much solitude or engagement as you wish. What's most interesting about the places featured in the article is that while some are linked with Roman Catholic establishments, many are linked with other kinds of centres such as Buddhist communities, spiritual centres and even health spas. Solitary contemplation is clearly valued by practitioners of many spiritual traditions and none, and almost all religious faiths incorporate strong contemplative components.

In a Wexford bookshop I look at *The Seven Storey Mountain*, the auto-biography of Thomas Merton, an American Trappist monk, theologian, mystic, poet and social activist. Merton was Catholic but had an interest in other religions. He devoted serious time and application to under-standing many spiritual traditions and saw great value in aspects of Buddhism, Hinduism, Jainism, Taoism and Sufism. As he noted, there are common features across many faiths, and contemplative practice is, perhaps, the most prominent commonality of all. I must actually read that book sometime, as opposed to simply looking at it in bookshops.

–

Monday 7 August

I have a dim memory of reading somewhere about a Buddhist monk who was so absorbed in meditation that small animals ate his toes and he did not budge. I can't track down the story now, but as I sit on a quayside mooring bollard in Wexford this morning with my eyes gently shut, a dog lollops up and starts licking my hand. Unlike the monk in the story, I open my eyes immediately and pet the gorgeous, enthusi-astic dog, who then licks my face. There would be nothing enlightened about ignoring this! I end up quite wet.

It's our last day in Wexford. En route back to Dublin, we come across Buddhist prayer flags in the National Botanic Gardens in Kilmacur-ragh. The colourful flags mark the bicentenary of the birth of Sir Joseph Dalton Hooker, a British botanist, explorer and director of the Royal Botanical Gardens in Kew. Hooker visited Ireland and travelled exten-sively around the globe, most famously to Nepal and India. Some of Hooker's seed collections from this expedition were sent to the National Botanic Gardens in Glasnevin, Dublin in 1850. Seedlings were distrib-uted to Kilmacurragh in 1862 and the collection still flourishes in the garden. Buddhist prayer flags from the Bhutan and Sikkim Himalaya flutter here today to commemorate Hooker's life, work and travels.

Tuesday 8 August

Following on from my journal entry about Thomas Merton, I've been reading online about Sufism or 'mystical Islam'. This is a recurring theme. Here are two interesting, thought-provoking Sufi quotes from Hazrat Inayat Khan, with distinct Buddhist undertones:

> *There are two aspects of individual harmony: the harmony between body and soul, and the harmony between individuals. All the tragedy in the world, in the individual and in the multitude, comes from lack of harmony. And harmony is best given by producing harmony in one's own life.*
>
> *The first lesson to learn is to resign oneself to the little difficulties in life, not to hit out at everything one comes up against. If one were able to manage this one would not need to cultivate great power; even one's presence would be healing.*

That final quote is, perhaps, the more challenging on a day-to-day level: it is easy to get caught up in minor unfairness and miss what is important – both the joys of life and the major injustices that merit attention. There is much that I admire in Sufism, and much of great interest in the history and culture of the Middle East.

–

Wednesday 9 August

I sit with continual distraction owing chiefly to restlessness. Buddhism speaks of 'five hindrances' to meditation: sensory desire (*kāmacchanda*), which relates to the desire to seek happiness through the senses of sight, sound, smell, taste and physical sensation; ill will (*vyāpāda*), which relates to anger, hatred, bitterness; torpor (*middha*), which is heaviness and dullness of body and mind, leading to inertia; restlessness and worry (*uddhacca* and *kukkucca*), which is being unable to calm the mind; and doubt (*vicikicchā*), which is a lack of trust or conviction.

Restlessness is the big one: the desire to keep on doing things, keep moving. Restlessness of mind, in the form of worry, is especially pernicious: should I be using this time to do something else? Why am

I meditating? Did I forget to do this or that? Worry is as endless as it is pointless.

–

Thursday 10 August

I'm reading (or, rather, glancing through) *Meditations* by Marcus Aurelius, who wrote about Stoic philosophy, which has much in common with Buddhism: 'You have power over your mind – not outside events. Realise this, and you will find strength.' And: 'If you are distressed by anything external, the pain is not due to the thing itself, but to your estimate of it; and this you have the power to revoke at any moment.'

Aurelius touches on Buddhist themes of mindfulness, gratitude and happiness: 'When you arise in the morning think of what a privilege it is to be alive, to think, to enjoy, to love ...' And: 'Never let the future disturb you. You will meet it, if you have to, with the same weapons of reason which today arm you against the present.' And: 'Very little is needed to make a happy life; it is all within yourself in your way of thinking.'

–

Friday 11 August

Fifteen minutes of moderate meditation today. I'm keeping going.

A patient complains about coverage of mental health issues in the media. Jasmine is a sixty-year old woman with severe depression. She has twice made serious attempts to kill herself. Jasmine has been well now for over three years with a combination of lifestyle changes (more exercise, improved eating habits, no alcohol), psychological therapy and antidepressant medication. She needs all three strands of treatment, she says. And, in her case, I agree with her 100 per cent. At this stage, Jasmine knows what she is talking about in ways that I can only imagine.

Jasmine is annoyed today not because mental health problems feature increasingly in the popular media (which is good) but because media tend to downplay or ignore serious mental illness, such as Jasmine's life-threatening depression. Much media coverage, she says, gives the impression that going running and changing your diet can fix everything, and you are somehow a failure if these measures prove insufficient. Sometimes, Jasmine says, running and broccoli are not enough.

Again, I agree with her that these (excellent) measures are sometimes not enough but I also point to increased media coverage of serious mental illness (e.g. schizophrenia, bipolar disorder) in recent times and increased recognition of the role medication can play for many. Jasmine remains unconvinced but I do see signs of positive change.

—

Saturday 12 August

Back to Marcus Aurelius: 'Reject your sense of injury and the injury itself disappears.' As with Buddhism, Aurelius especially values equanimity and seeing things as they really are: 'The first rule is to keep an untroubled spirit. The second is to look things in the face and know them for what they are.' In the end, 'our life is what our thoughts make it'.

—

Sunday 13 August

Buddhism is a pacifist philosophy but it is not passive. Buddhism abhors violence but requires rigorous, active, sustained effort to achieve its goals. The degree of effort needed is, perhaps, ironic because one of the goals of Buddhist practice is a quiet mind. This is also the goal of many other philosophical systems: even the Roman politician Marcus Tullius Cicero, who was not even vaguely Buddhist, stated that 'a happy life consists in tranquillity of mind'. Buddhism asserts that tranquillity of mind is largely a habit and can be cultivated through dedicated, slow, steady practice.

My meditation project is a sustained effort to achieve 'tranquillity of mind' based largely on Buddhist techniques, although many other spiritual and philosophical traditions also contribute. The mind has a tendency to jump from topic to topic, to disturb its natural tranquillity to such an extent that we come to believe that restlessness rather than tranquillity is the natural resting state of the mind. It is not. Tranquillity is the natural resting state of mind. It is worth rediscovering this belief to help restore the mind to its original, peaceful state.

–

Monday 14 August

Another perfect day, another imperfect meditation. I am getting better: more settled, less distracted, feeling more refreshed after meditating. My post-meditation irritability has diminished greatly. But this is very, very slow. It's a little like driving a car up an incline that is so gentle it does not feel like you are driving up a hill at all. But after some time, there comes a moment when you look around and realise that you have made progress. It is so gradual that you do not notice as it happens but at some point it all adds up and strikes you that you have been steadily progressing all along. Meditation is just like that: silent, slow, powerful.

–

Tuesday 15 August

Returning to this month's theme, 'right action', the fourth element in the noble eightfold path, I am reminded that this means not only 'abstaining from killing' but also 'abstaining from stealing' and 'abstaining from sexual misconduct'. The latter refers to celibacy for monks and, for lay people, refraining from adultery or other forms of sexual misconduct.

The prohibition on stealing is sometimes expressed as a prohibition on 'taking the not-given' and refers to stealing directly or by subterfuge. Both the intention and the act are important in determining what constitutes stealing because there are implications for *karma*, which, in Buddhism, basically means that good actions will produce good outcomes and bad ones will produce bad outcomes. Both the intention and the act matter for *karma*.

Applying the prohibition on stealing seems fairly straightforward at first but can become complex in practice. Clearly, few people actually rob banks or steal things in shops, but some people manipulate others disproportionately in such a way as to elicit things they want, blurring the lines between stealing, manipulating and negotiating. This can be very subtle and can involve unconscious use of pre-existing power relations to make unreasonable demands of others, demands they cannot resist. In this way, a given act might not initially look like stealing but the intention underpinning it might. Careful self-awareness is vital if one is not to behave in this fashion.

–

Wednesday 16 August

I meditate for twenty minutes this morning, five minutes longer than usual. I am hesitant because I do not want any step forward in my project to be followed by a step back. That's why I've been so reluctant to extend the duration of my meditation: I want each step forward to be clearly sustainable. There should be no turning back.

But today I impulsively decide to extend my daily meditation to twenty minutes after months of meditating steadily for fifteen. I have no idea why this should occur today as opposed to any other day, but there it is. Hopefully, this is a sustainable step forward, albeit a small one.

In the evening, I take a walk into Dublin city centre. It is starting to get dark a little earlier and the evening is cooler than before. Tourists wander about looking in guidebooks as often as they look around, gazing at mobile phones as often as they gaze at the city. I walk on, trying to be mindful.

–

Thursday 17 August

I'm on call: at work in the hospital during the day, covering for phone calls and psychiatric assessments during the night and back in to work tomorrow. It's a quiet night with just one or two assessments by the team. Psychiatry is an unusual part of medicine with a rhythm and pattern that differs in certain ways from much of the rest of the hospital. But in other ways, acute psychiatry slots right into the hospital system: emergency presentations occur at all hours of the day and night, treatment can be delivered as an outpatient or an inpatient, and unexpected complexities can crop up at any moment.

I am always struck by arguments that mental illness is solely a societal construct, a pejorative way of describing people who are simply different or do not fit in. There is more than a grain of truth in this for some people, but in my experience it is never the whole story or even the greater part of the story.

Whenever one meets a person who is very mentally ill, it is immediately clear that, whatever the cause is and whatever interpretive framework is used, this person is urgently in need of understanding, support and treatment. All of the philosophical and sociological theorising seems oddly irrelevant when one is confronted by a human being who is highly distressed, disturbed and suffering deeply.

In that moment, relieving suffering is the only thing that matters.

–

Friday 18 August

I sit for twenty minutes with moderate concentration and then read an article in *The New Yorker* titled 'American Nirvana' by Adam Gopnik, a writer I enjoy. Gopnik provides an interesting analysis of certain strands of contemporary Buddhist thought, especially in the US, along with a useful overview of key elements of Buddhist philosophy. The ideas underpinning Buddhism are certainly attractive: that we can control our minds with practice and meditation, and that compassion and kindness should inform our actions. Putting these ideas into practice is challenging but by no means impossible. 'Right effort' is required! I hope to think about 'right effort' a little more in October.

–

Saturday 19 August

This evening we go for a 'bat walk' in Castletown Demesne in Celbridge, just outside Dublin. This lovely event is organised by Kildare Bat Group as part of National Heritage Week. This evening is not our first bat walk and neither will it be our last. We are richly rewarded when dusk falls and we spot pipistrelle and Daubenton's bats swooping about at breakneck speed. Magic!

We arrive home to Dublin around 10.30 pm and meet a fox outside our front door. We sit in the car and the fox sits too, gazing at us steadily. As we gaze back, Trixie appears. Trixie has a love-hate relationship with the fox. Sometimes she seems to play with him and other times she chases him away. Buddhist Trixie tolerates the fox; catty Trixie defends her turf. Today, Trixie and the fox look at each other for a few minutes and then follow one another in and out of the bushes for a while. Finally, Trixie chases the fox away.

Having dealt with the intruder, Trixie comes into the house with us for the night. If we let her, Trixie would happily join us for a cup of tea – cold breakfast tea with milk, in her case. But we are advised that Trixie should drink only water and so she has some water and a treat before we all go to bed. That cat! I hope the fox is not traumatised.

–

Sunday 20 August

Some meditation early this morning is followed by a brave attempt to continue this weekend's nature theme. We head out to the woods at Kilternan for a walk. The rain sends us back to the car, however, so we go to the cinema to watch *An Inconvenient Sequel: Truth to Power*. It is the sequel to *An Inconvenient Truth*, a 2006 documentary that looked at Al Gore's campaign to educate the world about global warming.

Today's movie is compelling. Gore is an impressive speaker and thinker, and the film's message is a powerful one. Of course, it is easy to watch a movie like this but much more difficult to make changes in one's own life, especially in a society built on a pernicious cult of consumption. But that is no reason not to try: we leave the cinema filled with 'right resolve'.

Monday 21 August

Continuing with yesterday's ecological theme, Buddhism encourages deep respect for nature. Oneness with the natural world lies at the heart of much Buddhist philosophy.

In recent decades, Buddhism's concern with nature has been translated into the language of conservation and environmental awareness, consistent with yesterday's movie. But the roots of Buddhist engagement with nature are much older than this and run much deeper than the most recent western reawakening of environmental consciousness.

Sitting on my bookshelf, alongside many other partially read volumes, is a weighty tome titled *Buddhism and Ecology: The Interconnection of Dharma and Deeds*. 'Dharma' refers to Buddhist teachings, especially, in this case, teachings related to the environment. This fascinating book draws on ecological experiences in Thailand, Japan, India and the US, and explores themes such as the Buddhist philosophy of nature, Buddhism and animals and applications of Buddhist ecological worldviews.

As I glance through the book, a clipping I kept from *The Guardian* of 5 August 2011 slips out. The article recounts the release, by Tibetan Buddhists, of 534 lobsters into the Atlantic off Massachusetts on wheel-turning day of the Tibetan lunar calendar, which is the anniversary of the first sermon Buddha taught and a day when the merit for positive actions is multiplied. The monks in this report bought 272 kilograms of lobster from a seafood wholesaler and released them back into the ocean, rather than have them boiled and eaten.

The clipping has a lovely photo of a monk dropping a lobster into the ocean. The monk has a look of fierce concentration on his face. The lobster looks delighted (although it is admittedly difficult to tell with lobsters). In any case, it is respect for life that binds the scowling monk with the happy lobster, and binds all living creatures as one.

The Dalai Lama:

Whether they belong to more evolved species like humans or to simpler ones such as animals, all beings primarily seek peace, comfort, and security. Life is as dear to the mute animal as it is to any human being; even the simplest insect strives for protection from dangers that threaten its life. Just as each one of us wants to live and does not wish to die, so it is with all other creatures in the universe, though their power to effect this is a different matter.

–

Tuesday 22 August

I meditate quietly and better than usual: settled, gentle and moderately mindful. It is interesting how rewarding this is when it's working out. It is both simple and difficult at the same time. The instructions are ludicrously simple: sit, try to stay still, breathe, don't do anything else but don't worry too much if you get distracted – just refocus. But in practice it can be very difficult. To stop thinking and stop doing other things are the hardest parts. But the rewards of good practice are seen both in the moment and between times: less irritability, more calmness and greater awareness of the world.

–

Wednesday 23 August

Teachings about rebirth have been a prominent feature of Buddhist thought since the time of the Buddha. Buddha, on the night of his enlightenment, is said to have remembered over 100,000 previous lives. Rebirth has, however, continually generated significant debate, both in relation to specific aspects of rebirth theory and, in more recent times, the argument that rebirth is not a necessary feature of modern, 'agnostic', Buddhist thought.

There has also been considerable discussion about the search for empirical 'evidence' to support the teaching of rebirth, especially evidence based on studies of spontaneous and hypnotically recovered memories of past lives; that is, people who report remembering specific details about their 'past lives'.

In the end, it is clear that the diversity of sources, findings and interpretations of research about 'past lives' highlights the need for a considered, skilful approach to the topic. It is also important to bear in mind that the absence of evidence does not imply that a phenomenon does not occur; for some phenomena, it may be extraordinarily difficult to prove they occur. Nonetheless, it is still important to critically evaluate available evidence. On this basis, cases of 'spontaneous memory of past lives' derived through hypnotic regression appear particularly unconvincing, owing chiefly to enhanced possibilities for conscious and unconscious distortion, elaboration and amplification as a result of hypnosis.

The literature on this topic also suggests that it may be useful to interpret the search for empirical evidence about rebirth in conjunction with the search for other forms of 'evidence', which may be valued within certain spiritual contexts, such as meditative and/or spiritual experience, to which Buddhist tradition attaches great value.

The optimal interpretation of this evidence, both 'empirical' and 'experiential', is likely to relate to the level of skilfulness employed when engaging with Buddhist thought in general and the extent to which thinkers and practitioners maintain due regard for other areas of Buddhist tradition and practice. Overall, the 'empirical' approach has proven a controversial adjunct to, rather than a replacement for, a more individual approach to this theme, rooted in meditative experience, cultivation of mindfulness and generally skilful engagement with broader Buddhist themes relating to spiritual thought and practice.

–

Thursday 24 August

Meditation: twenty minutes of distraction and occasional calm. Not so bad.

–

Friday 25 August

I see *A Ghost Story*, starring Rooney Mara, Casey Affleck and some ghosts. The movie is an odd, pleasing, unpredictable thing. The ghosts seem sad.

I think a bit about ghosts. They definitely exist inside our heads. Do they exist as separate independent entities also, outside our heads? If Buddhism teaches that there is 'no self', are we ghosts?

Saturday 26 August

Back to this month's theme in my meditation project, 'right action', the fourth element in the noble eightfold path. It's been a mixed bag for August so far. I didn't actively kill anything but I ate meat, so I didn't truly abstain from killing. And while I didn't quite steal anything, some would say that the wealth enjoyed by rich countries like Ireland stands in such contrast with much of the developing world that it should be called stealing. Still, I had heightened awareness of right action during the month of August and I kept ill-intent to a minimum, so that's a start. Meditation has certainly made me calmer, which helps too.

–

Sunday 27 August

This morning: a two-hour kayak trip on the Grand Canal. It is unexpectedly sunny, leafy, quiet, contemplative – and wet!

–

Monday 28 August

This month's book is *The Art of Buddhism: An Introduction to its History and Meaning* by Denise Patry Leidy, which covers Buddhist art from early pillars and stupas (hemispherical structures containing relics) right up to the nineteenth century. I have leafed through this book many times over the years and am invariably moved most deeply by the stone images, such as those at Bayon temple in Cambodia: the faces are strong, striking and peaceful. I would love to visit Angkor Wat, the largest religious monument in the world. It was originally a Hindu temple dedicated to the god Vishnu but it gradually became a Buddhist centre of worship during the twelfth century.

For now, though, until I make that trip, I have this book to enjoy. I must meditate more. And travel more.

–

Tuesday 29 August

Quietly busy at work but with twenty minutes' meditation sandwiched in at some point. I'm also making progress with running over these past few weeks: I've been getting out for a run twice a week, for twenty to twenty-five minutes each time. Good, good.

But I must be honest: I dislike running. I try to do it twice a week solely because I believe it's good for my physical and psychological health. I do not enjoy it in the slightest. There are endless articles in newspapers and magazines and online detailing the euphoric highs that people describe after going for a run. The enjoyment. The rush of energy. The transcendental joy. But I experience none of that. Zero. I dislike every single step and, on a bad day, I deeply resent the time I spend running.

–

Wednesday 30 August
Trixie spends much of this morning sitting looking at me as I sit, have breakfast, and then work on the computer. When I get home from work she is still sitting there, calm and mysterious as the Sphinx. There is much to learn from that cat.

–

Thursday 31 August
And so August ends. I am now two-thirds of the way though my year of daily meditation. On the plus side, I have meditated steadily and am somewhat calmer, more aware of my mental states. On the minus side, I still have this niggling feeling that I have not progressed nearly enough. I also worry that I'm devoting too much time to this journal and not enough time to proper spiritual or contemplative practice.

Also, I think that I worry too much. And far too often, I worry about worrying. Is that cause for further worry?

I eat cake. This month: a mini lemon meringue pie with a pastry base, lemon custard filling and irresistible meringue topping. I've always loved meringue so the guests who gave us this cake earlier in the week certainly knew what they were doing.

It's another end-of-month sugar rush for me. And I love it.

September

—

RIGHT LIVELIHOOD

In which autumn arrives and I meditate. I listen to Buddhist chant and reflect on an array of topics including (but not limited to) memorable Buddhist book titles, meditation instructions, writing books, Tibetan refugees in India, Buddhist politics and this month's theme, 'right livelihood'. I return yet again to Sufism and various books (read and unread) about contemplative practice: so many books, so little meditation! Trixie appears, disappears and reappears with neither compunction nor explanation. Also featuring this month: Sufi music at high volume in the car and a stay at a retreat centre, where I try to be more contemplative, with mixed results. Conspicuous by their absence: genuine meditative progress, true reflective engagement, and – of course – enlightenment. I keep going.

Friday 1 September

Another month. It is definitely autumn now: colder, crisper. I wonder (during my meditation, unfortunately) if I should be meditating for longer periods by this stage. I try to clear my mind to refocus but it proves difficult. Thoughts keep entering my head and I am tempted to stop meditating and jot down a few reminders about various things. I resist this temptation and by the end of my twenty minutes I've completely forgotten what it was I was going to remind myself about. I wish I could say that I simply smile and move on with my life, but I don't. I remain vaguely troubled that I've forgotten things I should have noted down. I've no idea what they are now. It's an unsettling start to a new month. Still, on we go. Onward, onward.

–

Saturday 2 September

We visit Áras an Uachtaráin. I visited many years ago and recall seeing a photograph of a previous president, Erskine Hamilton Childers, meeting the Dalai Lama there in 1973. There's no sign of the photograph at the Áras today and I wonder was I mistaken. Later, a quick internet search confirms that such a visit occurred on 10 October 1973. I even find a delightful video of the meeting on YouTube, featuring a young Dalai Lama visiting Áras an Uachtaráin as part of his European tour. There's something intrinsically inviting about Buddhist thought, which underpins my meditation project and much of this diary, and accounts for the extraordinary popularity of the Dalai Lama – even in 1970s Ireland. Perhaps I'm talking about truth.

–

Sunday 3 September

I have a growing library of books about meditation and Buddhism, often with splendid titles like *Wherever You Go, There You Are: Mindfulness Meditation for Everyday Life* and *After the Ecstasy, the Laundry: How the Heart Grows Wise on the Spiritual Path*.

I am not especially influenced by any single teacher or writer. In fact, I tend to be suspicious of those who are overly invested in any single teacher or practitioner of Buddhism (or anything else). Some voices are especially compelling, like those of Jon Kabat-Zinn, Jack Kornfield or Mark Epstein, author of *Thoughts Without a Thinker: Psychotherapy from a Buddhist Perspective* and *Psychotherapy Without the Self: A Buddhist Perspective*. Others seem more interested in developing their own schools of practice or corners of Buddhism, rather than contributing to shared experience and spiritual advancement. These people are to be avoided. It is good and necessary that there are many voices – there are many listeners.

But I also have too many books in my house and the clutter they create seems inconsistent with the clarity and weightlessness of Buddhism. I should prioritise, decant and detach from physical books. The real issue, of course, is mental rather than physical clutter. Thus, meditation.

–

Monday 4 September

Trixie is especially impish today. She darts around the house at high speed, sits quietly for a few moments and then darts around the house again. There is no understanding her.

–

Tuesday 5 September

Over the years I've accumulated a small collection of CDs relating to meditation and Buddhism. Many of these are sets of meditation instructions that I have never found helpful. I prefer to read meditation guidance in a book or on a website, commit it to memory and then practise without interruption. I'm also influenced by an 'introduction to meditation' course I did over ten years ago, which still shapes my paltry day-to-day efforts.

So, leaving meditation instruction CDs to one side, my favourite Buddhist CD is *Tibetan Chants, Buddhist Meditation* by Lama Karta. I return to it repeatedly because it features a single monk chanting: no musical accompaniment, no bells, no chimes, no birdsong, no whale sounds, no dolphin song, no panpipes and none of the other additions that sometimes feature alongside Buddhist chant. I like plain, unvarnished chant and this CD delivers it clearly, directly and well.

Lama Karta's voice is gravelly and full of character. I have absolutely no idea what he is saying. I know I could find out (there's actually a little booklet with the CD, now that I look at it), but I value greatly a listening experience that is unmediated by language: it is less cognitive, more experiential. I need more of that.

And for another experience of a direct nature, unmediated by language, I can today recommend Pickle, a North Indian restaurant on Dublin's Camden Street. Fauzi chicken wings followed by farmer's butter chicken. There are – literally – *no words*.

–

Wednesday 6 September

Only yesterday I waxed lyrical about Buddhist chant, but today I must admit to listening to the *Rough Guide to Sufi Music* on repeat at high volume in the car. Sufism is fascinating and affecting. My booming Sufi music gets some strange looks from other motorists at the traffic lights but it's well worth it.

–

Thursday 7 September

I try to cut down on the booming Sufi music a little. It's time for some quiet time. I have a busy but controlled day at work, seeing patients, attending meetings, catching up with emails.

I see a woman called Mary. She has been referred by her GP because she seems anxious. Mary arrives in a flustered state. I say little during our interview and just let her story unfold at its own pace. She settles down after a while. In essence, Mary is complaining of tension, headaches and poor sleep. She is agitated and irritated much of the time. She often feels her heart beating rapidly. Mary tells me she looked all of this up and concluded that she has anxiety. Her appetite and energy are poor and she has difficulty concentrating her mind at work, but lies in bed at night with thoughts about work racing through her head.

Mary is stressed. We often use the word 'stress' to describe day-to-day pressures that keep us motivated and performing well. But things can get out of hand when the demands on us consistently exceed our resources, and our bodies enter a state of constant high stress. Stress becomes our new normal. We cannot turn off. Mary needs to step back a little from work and take some active measures to reduce her stress. We talk about this for a while and Mary makes some excellent suggestions herself, much better and more specific to her life than anything I could have come up with.

So often we know what we need to do but we simply don't manage to do it. In a way, it's just like meditation: I've no doubts about the theory but I falter with the practice.

–

Friday 8 September
This month's theme is 'right livelihood', the fifth element of the noble eightfold path. Right livelihood means living in a way that does not cause harm, is honest and skilful and is ethically positive. One should avoid 'wrong livelihood', which means avoiding accumulating excessive possessions and not cheating, harming, killing and any other activities considered unskilful and unenlightened in Buddhist thought.

Broadly, anyone can achieve right livelihood although it's difficult to see how someone who works directly with killing can do so (for example, an abattoir employee). But it would be hypocritical of anyone who eats meat to denounce people who work in abattoirs for killing sentient beings, because eating meat makes us an integral part of a chain of events centred on the killing of sentient beings for food. The fundamental problem lies with us, the meat-eaters, not them.

These tasks are not easy, especially if they involve changing ingrained habits. But the teaching of right livelihood suggests that everyone should strive to move in this direction if we are to attain greater wisdom, compassion, understanding and enlightenment.

Saturday 9 September

A lovely day: a little early-morning meditation, a couple of hours of work, various family activities and then a visit to a Michelin-starred restaurant for a special occasion. I have limited patience with fussy, cheffy food: drizzles of this and hints of that, all thinly spread over enormous plates making the entire spectacle impossible to eat. I am absolutely allergic to restaurants where staff need to ask: 'Has anyone explained our concept to you?' And I struggle with food served on slates, pieces of wood, tiny shopping trolleys, collections of twigs, etc. Whatever happened to plates? Plates are brilliant.

Much high-end dining manages to both demand attention and be the opposite of mindful eating. It encourages obsession with flourishes and flights of fancy, a far cry from the mindful asceticism of Buddhism. Simplicity is key: appropriately sized plates are simple, straightforward and highly effective for the task of conveying food. They cannot be improved upon. Plates are simple and therefore perfect.

–

Sunday 10 September

Do Buddhism and politics mix? Buddhism certainly provides a clear framework for political action centred on compassion. And compassion is not the vague, weak value it is sometimes portrayed as, but a robust, assertive value that challenges the fundamentals of adversarial political discourse and calls for deep awareness of suffering on the basis that the suffering of others is continuous with our own. We suffer as one.

I've especially enjoyed two books on the theme of Buddhism and politics. The first is *Mindful Politics: A Buddhist Guide to Making the World a Better Place* edited by Melvin McLeod and featuring contributions from, among others, Thích Nhat Hanh, the Dalai Lama, Pema Chödrön, Joseph Goldstein and Rita M. Gross. This volume presents a good mix of perspectives on Buddhism and politics and hangs together pretty well as a unified entity.

The second book has the unlikely title *A Mindful Nation: How a Simple Practice Can Help Us Reduce Stress, Improve Performance, and Recapture the American Spirit*. US Congressman Tim Ryan places considerable emphasis on the benefits of mindfulness for society in general and this is why I like this book so much: his arguments convey a palpable sense of community that is both highly consistent with the essence of Buddhist thought and much needed in many societies today. Both of these books reward careful attention and would, ideally, nudge me into political action rooted in Buddhist values.

–

Monday 11 September

I think about possible titles for this journal. *Just Sit? My Year of Meditating Daily and How It Changed My Life? My Year of Meditating Badly and How It Did Not Change My Life? That Cat!? When There Is No Self, There Is No Selfie?*

In one sense, I'm not entirely certain why this journal *needs* a title, but I feel it does. Initially more of a distraction than a help, the journal has slowly become a key part of the process, prompting reflection and further thought between meditation sits. At this stage, it seems like it needs a title to reflect its role. How about *The Doctor Who Sat for A Year?*

–

Tuesday 12 September

Busy day at work. But then, there is no such thing as a quiet day. Whenever a space opens up in my schedule, it is immediately filled with new tasks, phone calls, meetings, priorities – all of the thousands of little things that make up the building blocks of modern life. I meditate badly somewhere in the middle. I can never decide if it's better to wait until a quiet time to meditate, or if I should make the conscious effort required to clear a space to meditate in the midst of the daily storm; that is, make a point of trying to meditate during a busy period and therefore (hopefully) demonstrate mastery over the flurried hurry that characterises so much of the day.

In the end, I decide that a balance of both approaches is useful, not least because I will become frustrated unless I do at least some meditating at times when I am likely to succeed. There is no point setting myself up to fail *every* time.

Wednesday 13 September

I decide to go on a short retreat starting next Sunday. This will not be a structured retreat: there are no scheduled meditation sessions or other 'mandatory' activities. In a concession to realism, I select a retreat centre with internet access so that I can clear my emails each day and then focus on meditating and just 'being' (rather than 'doing'). The centre also offers quiet walks and solitary reflective time. As it is a Roman Catholic monastery, there will be opportunity to attend liturgies in the church: matins, vespers, compline, etc. I like that kind of thing. I've no idea why.

I've been thinking about doing something like this for many years. It will hopefully help with my desire to spend more time meditating in a focused way and add a new dimension to my meditation project. I've been prattling on about all kinds of diverse things (movies, books, the cat, incidental ephemera) in this journal for many months. Perhaps it's finally time to focus on meditating.

I meditate fitfully, with conscious effort rather than composure.

–

Thursday 14 September

Buddha: 'Meditation brings wisdom; lack of meditation leaves ignorance. Know well what leads you forward and what holds you back, and choose the path that leads to wisdom.' On we go: keeping on keeping on.

I see Mary again. She is still stressed and disappointed that she has succeeded in doing 'only' around 50 per cent of what she resolved to do last week: speaking with her boss, leaving work promptly at 5 pm, cutting down her alcohol intake and attending her weekly yoga class. I tell her the truth: succeeding with 50 per cent of what you resolve to do is *amazing*. She is genuinely doing great.

–

Friday 15 September

This month's book is *A Doctor in Little Lhasa: One Year in Dharamsala with the Tibetans in Exile* by Timothy Holtz, who spent a year working as a volunteer doctor in Delek Hospital in Dharamsala, India, where Tibetan Buddhist refugees congregate.

Holtz provides an especially clear picture of the realities of day-to-day life with the refugees and demonstrates, again and again, how the problems presenting at the hospital find their roots in social conditions within refugee settlements.

From a Buddhist perspective, the book emphasises not only the plight of Tibetan Buddhist refugees in India but also the power of Holtz's selfless approach to medical and social care, at once dedicated and passionate, humble and humbling.

A Doctor in Little Lhasa is a fascinating read that I believe should be mandatory for medical students and everyone involved in clinical or social care. But there are so many books and I spend so much time reading! Perhaps I'd be better off meditating more and reading less?

–

Saturday 16 September

I am, perhaps, adding to my 'so many books, so little meditation!' problem by writing another book myself. This one, which I've already mentioned, will be titled *Mental Health in Ireland: The Complete Guide for Patients, Families, Health Care Professionals and Everyone Who Wants To Be Well*. The book is intended as a pragmatic guide to mental health problems and their solutions, aimed at anyone who has ever felt overwhelmed by their problems and situation, or developed a mental illness.

I've been meaning to write this book for several years. Writing in the evenings after work is not quite mindful but it is certainly settling. Essentially, I am writing about problems and solutions that I see in my working life, so setting it all down on paper makes a great deal of sense. It does not feel like an additional task, just an extension of my usual activities. I like the rhythm of writing: the flow of words, the reading, the editing, the re-reading, the re-editing, and so forth. There is something reassuring and iterative about the process, almost soothing. Perhaps it is mindful.

Sunday 17 September

Off I go to my meditation retreat. I feel a little bad just heading away like this but if I am to take my meditation project seriously, I need to take this step. I arrive in the evening and immediately there are a number of problems. Meditation teachers would call them 'hindrances' but to me they are just problems – and quite disturbing ones at that.

Number one: I cannot use the internet in my room. I know that one should seek to get away ('retreat') from the internet and the like, but I settle down much better when I've cleared my email. I *like* the internet; I'm not a slave to it, but I do like it.

Number two: the curtains are white and thin. I invariably wake incredibly early (4 or 5 am) if my bedroom is not as dark as a deep, deep cave. And even then, I generally wake before 6 am.

Number three: there is absolutely no mobile phone cover, so I cannot let my family know I got here safely. These are all annoyances. Perhaps I should treat them as hindrances to meditation (reflect on them, work through them, etc. etc.) but right now they are annoyances.

On the plus side, the retreat centre is certainly in a striking location, although I have always been unmoved by the immediate location of places where I stay. I prefer to stay somewhere comfortable and functional that looks out onto a car park rather than somewhere with nice views but no wifi.

I decide to make the best of things and I attend vespers at 6 pm, followed by supper (in merciful silence), and then compline (night prayer), a little after 8 pm. It is all very monastic. I have always found monasticism interesting, be it in Umberto Eco's *The Name of the Rose* or the films *Of Gods and Men* and *Into Great Silence*, the latter being one of my favourite movies of all times: unexpected, intense and very, very moving.

This evening, vespers, too, is affecting, gentle and powerful. I'm starting to warm to this place. Oddly, I am the only male staying in the guesthouse. After night prayer, as I type in this journal, three of my fellow houseguests sit outside the window of my room, chatting:

'It's very quiet here.'

'Yes, not a sound.'

'It's really lovely and peaceful.'

'No traffic, nobody talking.'

'Yes, nothing at all.'

'Just lovely and quiet.'

'It's great to get away from the noise and the chatter.'

'It really is.'

'No chatter at all.'

'I just love the quiet.'

'It's very quiet here.'

'No talking.'

'So peaceful.'

This goes on for around half an hour but it is peaceful enough in its own way and eventually it ends.

—

Monday 18 September

I wake early after a poor night's sleep. I trot off to the church for matins and lauds (morning prayer). It is a dark, chilly morning but the hushed church is quiet and restful after my restless night. In the distance a dog barks from time to time but there is no other sound. Morning prayer is not unlike vespers and compline: contemplative, prayerful, understated. There is a mix of prayer, chant and song. Afterwards, it is bright outside and a brave sun makes an appearance.

The rest of the day has a monastic structure to it: mass around midday, vespers in the early evening, supper in silence in the refectory and so forth. I take a walk around the grounds and sneak out to buy some newspapers, which I drive several miles to get.

I meditate for the usual twenty minutes but fail to meditate for longer: I am too occupied with attending the various services in the church, walking in the fields and using the solitude to revise research papers. The internet situation limits my computer activity but, even so, I still do not meditate for any longer than I usually do. Then again, longer meditation was not one of my explicit goals in coming here; general peacefulness was the main idea.

That said, I am more *generally* meditative today or, more accurately, *generally contemplative* in my demeanour: more measured, steady and (despite a poor night's sleep) rested. This general shift is, perhaps, more important than achieving longer meditation sits? More important than simply notching up meditation time? Or am I just kidding myself again? Making up new excuses for not meditating?

I go for another walk to think about it.

–

Tuesday 19 September

I'm not exactly living like a monk for these three days but this is probably as close as I'm likely to get. Again, today starts with matins and lauds in the early morning, followed by mass, vespers and compline. I wonder what is it like to be a monk. How soon does the rhythm of monastic life come to feel natural and even inevitable? Does the monastic day eventually feel just as stressful to a monk as my days feel to me when I'm at home, going to work and doing a dozen different things all at once?

Again, I walk in the grounds, pop out for newspapers and work. It's my last full day at the retreat centre. I am enjoying my time here. It has really carved out a space in day-to-day life and given me some time for pausing and thinking. I haven't actually thought anything particularly important or reached specific conclusions during my stay here, but it has been a thoughtful few days nonetheless. Being thoughtful without thoughts? Definite echoes of Buddhism there.

–

Wednesday 20 September

And so I hit the road to Dublin. I take away this morning's matins and lauds, the dark, crisp autumn dawn, the hushed tones of the monks, the chant and all other kinds of memories. Soon I am on the motorway zipping back home. After the ethereal beauty of the monastery, Barack

Obama Plaza, with its petrol pumps, fast food and tinny music, seems like another world. But it's my world. I adjust rapidly and push onwards.

–

Thursday 21 September

I know I should eat less meat so as not to support killing and to improve my health. But I'd be lying if I said I wasn't hungry for a burger after my three days at the retreat centre. I've some work to do on this yet.

–

Friday 22 September

'The foot feels the foot when it feels the ground.' Did Buddha really say this? I have a go with my foot outside the house. I think my foot feels the ground. Or, to put it another way, if there was no ground, my foot would feel nothing. Perhaps I'm missing something here.

–

Saturday 23 September

More from Buddha (and he makes it all sound simple here): 'Do not dwell in the past, do not dream of the future, concentrate the mind on the present moment.' Right, then.

–

Sunday 24 September

I'm still mulling over various aspects of my retreat, especially some of the Bible readings that were new to me. I hunted around today and found this rather apocalyptic passage from the *Book of Ezekiel* (1) which unnerved me with its vividness as I listened to it last week in the hushed, darkened church:

I looked, and I saw a windstorm coming out of the north – an immense cloud with flashing lightning and surrounded by brilliant light. The centre of the fire looked like glowing metal, and in the fire was what looked like four living creatures. In appearance their form was human, but each of them had four faces and four wings. Their legs were straight; their feet were like those of a calf and gleamed like burnished bronze. Under their wings on their four sides they had human hands. All four of them had faces and wings, and the wings of one touched the wings of another. Each one went straight ahead; they did not turn as they moved.

Their faces looked like this: Each of the four had the face of a human being, and on the right side each had the face of a lion, and on the left the face of an ox; each also had the face of an eagle. Such were their faces. They each had two wings spreading out upward, each wing touching that of the creature on either side; and each had two other wings covering its body. Each one went straight ahead. Wherever the spirit would go, they would go, without turning as they went. The appearance of the living creatures was like burning coals of fire or like torches. Fire moved back and forth among the creatures; it was bright, and lightning flashed out of it. The creatures sped back and forth like flashes of lightning.

–

Monday 25 September

Back to meditating in the usual fashion today: twenty minutes with minimal distraction. I sit upstairs with the sun streaming in through the window. It is warm on my face. It feels like a physical thing. It is. I am.

–

Tuesday 26 September

I spend part of the evening looking through meditation instructions on the internet. I've no idea why. I do not lack for instruction! What I lack is application. But maybe I also lack self-belief – the belief that if I stick to my practice I will eventually make progress. Self-belief can become excessive at times but a certain amount is necessary in order to persevere with anything. Chinese philosopher Lao Tzu: 'Because one believes in oneself, one doesn't try to convince others. Because one is content with oneself, one doesn't need others' approval. Because one accepts oneself, the whole world accepts him or her.' Mark Twain was saltier but no less direct: 'The worst loneliness is to not be comfortable with yourself.'

Wednesday 27 September

Once again, Trixie appears, disappears and reappears without explanation. That cat seems entirely accepting of herself. Lao Tzu would be pleased, and so would Mark Twain. But do I know this for certain? Maybe Trixie is tormented by inner doubt and simply does not show it? It seems unlikely. I don't imagine that any creature that sleeps so much can be especially uncomfortable with herself. I wonder if she dreams?

–

Thursday 28 September

While this journal is primarily concerned with Buddhist meditation, it is worth re-emphasising that meditation is by no means an exclusively Buddhist pursuit. Contemplative practice features in virtually all religions and spiritual traditions. For Christians, meditation is a form of prayer that deepens awareness of God and His message. St John Climacus, a sixth- to seventh-century Christian monk, emphasised that 'meditation gives birth to perseverance, and perseverance ends in perception, and what is accomplished with perception cannot easily be rooted out'. The same can be said of Buddhist meditation: perseverance with meditation helps the practitioner to see things as they really are and to develop a skill set, approach to life and set of values that are not easily extinguished.

–

Friday 29 September

Today's meditation is not great: I am distracted by everything from my own breathing to sounds outside the door to long-forgotten details of things I need to do at work. I try to let my intrusive thoughts float past like clouds in the sky but I make little progress. I finish up in a frustrated state, haunted by one of my earliest recurring problems with contemplative practice: post-meditation irritability. There is nothing for it now but to try again tomorrow.

Saturday 30 September

I meditate for twenty minutes with moderate effort and moderate effect. I am three-quarters of the way through my year of daily meditation. What have I learned? Nothing to write home about, really, and certainly nothing I could not have read in a book. But I have, I suppose, *experienced* that (a) meditation is both simple and difficult at the same time, and I seem to have reached a plateau at twenty minutes per day; (b) meditation gets easier when you do it every day; and (c) my progress has been consistently imperfect over the past nine months: *duhkha* everywhere!

On the plus side, September saw me spend three days in a retreat centre and even though it didn't exactly turbocharge my meditation practice, it did propel me into a more contemplative, mindful, self-aware state. While the centre I chose was not a Buddhist establishment, there was more than enough commonality of practice and intent to ensure relevance and benefit.

All told, I'm happy just to be still motoring along. I enjoy some end-of-month cake. This month, I have some apple tart baked by a neighbour and given as thanks for lending him a stepladder. There was no need for the tart but I'm delighted to have it now. I disliked apple tart as a child but love it as an adult. I've become less selective about cake.

Today, I eat a slice of tart and renew my determination to keep going with my meditation. Simply that: keep going.

October

—

RIGHT EFFORT

In which I meditate moderately well and reflect on this month's theme, 'right effort': that is, keeping my motivation right and remaining positive even when outcomes are initially disappointing or even paradoxically bad. I think again about the significance of self-immolation in Buddhist tradition: self-immolation inflicts suffering and does not respect life but, on the other hand, there is no doubting the good intentions of the Buddhist monks, nuns and others who self-immolate. Is that right effort? Surely not. Other topics crop up repeatedly (chiefly when I should be deep in contemplation): meditation postures (especially sitting), the nature of this journal (unclear), the possibility of titling this journal *The Scowling Monk and the Happy Lobster* (long story), and any number of plays, books and other distracting thoughts. Overall it is a good month of daily meditating, even if my progress is not everything I might wish for: *duhkha* everywhere! I must go on.

Sunday 1 October

I sit with calm, wintery deliberation.

—

Monday 2 October

Buddha: 'Whatever has the nature of arising has the nature of ceasing.'
I especially like this quotation. All is change. Things that please us, they
will pass. Things that annoy us, they will pass. This advice, it will pass.

—

Tuesday 3 October

I read over this entire journal to date. It is a bracing experience. What
on earth am I doing?

I'm a bit worried. The journal gives no sense of whether or not
I'm making real, sustained progress. On the other hand, it is an
honest reflection of my year so far. The meditative process has been a
non-linear one. It has been more dimensional than linear, just like time
spent meditating is qualitatively different from time spent doing other
things. A meditation sit is not *just* twenty minutes in a quiet room; it
is something different, with a very different quality. I can't put better
words on this at the moment and maybe I never will.

—

Wednesday 4 October

'Right effort' is this month's theme in my year-long project, the sixth
element of the noble eightfold path. What is right effort? Buddhist
literature says that it is all about 'will':

*And what is right effort? Here, the monk arouses his will, puts forth effort,
generates energy, exerts his mind, and strives to prevent the arising of evil
and unwholesome mental states that have not yet arisen. He arouses his will
... and strives to eliminate evil and unwholesome mental states that have
already arisen. He arouses his will ... and strives to generate wholesome
mental states that have not yet arisen. He arouses his will, puts forth effort,*

generates energy, exerts his mind, and strives to maintain wholesome mental states that have already arisen, to keep them free of delusion, to develop, increase, cultivate, and perfect them. This is called right effort.

–

Thursday 5 October

So how, exactly, should I practise right effort? How should I generate energy, exert my mind, strive 'to maintain wholesome mental states' and 'keep them free of delusion'? This is stirring stuff but it is not at all clear what I should actually *do.* I scan the internet for websites and advice about how to put right effort into operation in day-to-day life. As usual, I am bombarded with gushing advice, pay-per-view instruction videos and things that I can buy.

Overall, it seems that I need to eliminate ill will, anger and resentment and focus on positive mental states. Enthusiasm is important but must be tempered with patience and steadfastness, cheerfulness and honesty. Realism also needs to make an appearance to avoid disproportionate disappointment.

I think the key lies in keeping one's motivation and attitude positive, wholesome and directed towards Buddhist values (compassion, caring for others) even when outcomes do not always match up to the right effort put in. So that's it: right effort is about keeping my motivation right and remaining positive even when outcomes are initially disappointing or even paradoxical. How difficult can that be?

–

Friday 6 October

A busy, buzzy day. I do three radio interviews about my book *Mental Health in Ireland*. Over the course of the three interviews, I discuss all kinds of things with the presenters: specific mental illnesses, services for those affected, suicide and self-harm, support for families, and precisely what I'm trying to achieve with the book.

I like this kind of thing. I especially enjoy responding to the messages that listeners send in with particular questions or issues of concern. I hope that the book reaches some people who will benefit and that it helps spread reliable information about mental health to those who need it. This is a field calling out for common sense and pragmatism and that is the spirit in which I wrote the book. I hope it lives up to my goals.

In the afternoon I catch up with work and meditate briefly but find I am quite unsettled. I sit it out.

—

Saturday 7 October

The cat has started her seasonal killing spree. Trixie can appear with a dead mouse at any time of year, but especially around now, as the weather turns colder.

As a result, dead mice are deposited fairly frequently outside the back door over the past week or so. Today, to our collective horror, Trixie carries in a mouse that is still just about alive. We all get a fright as she bombs in through the cat flap with the poor creature wriggling in her mouth. She drops the mouse, which then drags itself under the piano.

We scour the internet to find advice about how to reduce the likelihood of Trixie bringing dead and dying creatures into the house. Last year she arrived home with a dead duckling. As usual there is no shortage of advice but much of it seems daft. The best is: (a) cats do not hunt owing to hunger, so overfeeding the cat (my strategy) will not solve the problem (drat!); (b) use a collar bell (which we already do); and (c) spend more time playing with the cat. Perhaps we can work on item (c).

Meanwhile there is unholy commotion until such time as we find the injured mouse, capture it and release it far from the house, in the hope that it does not die of its injuries. It scurries off. Perhaps we worry too much.

Sunday 8 October

We go cycling along the newly joined-up cycle path from Clontarf to Sutton and out towards Howth. It's a lovely route and the only difficulty is when groups of aggressive, lycra-clad cyclists come speeding along and want everyone else to clear out of their way. There seems to be less of that kind of boorishness today compared to our last visit here two or three months ago. Still, it's an occasional problem. This is regrettable: the cycle path is for everyone, so there will inevitably be children cycling slowly and tourists coasting along gently, much to the irritation of those cyclists who seem to think they are in the Tour de France. They are not. They are in Clontarf.

–

Monday 9 October

On 11 June 1963 the young Buddhist monk Thích Quảng Đức sat down in the lotus position at a traffic intersection in Saigon. A fellow monk poured gasoline over him and Thích Quảng Đức dropped a match on himself. He sat entirely motionless as he burned to death.

Thích Quảng Đức took his dramatic action to protest against the ongoing persecution of Buddhists by the regime of the Vietnamese President, Ngo Dinh Diem. Prior to his self-immolation, Thích Quảng Đức made a plea for religious equality:

I pray to Buddha to give light to President Ngo Dinh Diem, so that he will accept the five minimum requests of the Vietnamese Buddhists. Before closing my eyes to go to Buddha, I have the honour to present my words to President Diem, asking him to be kind and tolerant towards his people and enforce a policy of religious equality.

In response to Thích Quảng Đức's act of sacrifice, President Diem made a conciliatory statement but notwithstanding a resumption of negotiations between government and Buddhists, six more Buddhists died by self-cremation (i.e. self-burning). The conflict persisted for several more months and pressure grew on the Vietnamese government, both from the international community and from within Vietnam, owing, at least in part, to ongoing Buddhist suicides. Finally, in November 1963, President Diem was toppled by an army coup.

Self-immolation bears, at best, an uneasy relationship with Buddhist respect for life. Interestingly, there are notable points of similarity between considerations of self-harm and suicide in Buddhist and non-Buddhist traditions, including qualified acceptance of certain forms of self-harm, altruism as a motivation for suicide and self-immolation as a form of political protest. But there are also key differences, including the specific contexts in which certain forms of self-harm are partially accepted (for example, for altruistic reasons) and the predominant frameworks used to interpret such acts.

By definition, self-immolation refers to the sacrifice of one's own life, especially but not exclusively by fire (self-cremation); self-immolation may also involve drowning, starvation and feeding one's body to animals. Self-immolation is sometimes linked with specific political contexts, but, in contrast with suicide attacks, self-immolation aims to express disagreement and exert pressure, rather than inflict damage directly on others.

But self-immolation still inflicts pain and suffering on oneself and on others (for example, one's family and friends) and if my suffering is continuous with that of others (that is, there is no truly separate 'self'), then any increase in my suffering is unskilful. On the other hand, there is no doubting the good intentions of those who self-immolate (right effort?) and this contradiction makes self-immolation a profoundly paradoxical and, arguably, uniquely powerful act.

I will doubtless return to this troubling topic later this month, seeing as it's echoing around in my head again. I put it from my mind and try to sit.

Tuesday 10 October

Buddha: 'If with a pure mind a person speaks or acts, happiness follows them like a never-departing shadow.' Yes, but achieving a 'pure mind' is no easy feat!

At the clinic I see Shaun, a 52-year old man with bipolar disorder. Shaun was hospitalised twice with episodes of mania in his twenties. Mania occurs when a person's energy increases, their thoughts start racing and they lose the inhibitions that usually govern human behaviour. Shaun's episodes of mania were very disruptive indeed: he lost his job, got into debt and had significant problems with relationships.

At that time, Shaun commenced treatment with lithium, a medication commonly used to prevent recurrence of mania or depression in bipolar disorder. Shaun also attended counselling. The treatment worked. Shaun quickly reached a steady mental state and experienced no further mood episodes for several years.

After four years of stability, Shaun asked his then psychiatrist if his lithium could be stopped, as he had been well for quite a long period. His medication was carefully reduced at his request but he had a relapse of mania almost immediately. On that occasion, Shaun's illness was not as serious as before but was very disruptive nonetheless. His marriage ended. Shaun recommenced his lithium treatment promptly and has stayed on the medication ever since, in conjunction with counselling and various other treatments.

After two decades of stability, I am again discussing Shaun's treatment with him. He is adamant that he wants to stay on lithium. His episodes of mania in the past were so dramatic and disruptive that he still feels acutely traumatised by them. We talk about this at some length.

I have deep respect for Shaun's position on this. His descriptions of severe mania are very affecting. I cannot get them out of my head for the rest of the day.

Wednesday 11 October

Meditation is astonishingly difficult but great to do. This makes no logical sense. I always feel better afterwards – if not immediately, then later in the day. And I'm continually puzzled about why I do not do more of it. Why? What gives?

I think about this question a great deal today, including, ironically, when I should be meditating. And while I can come up with many reasons for this situation, I conclude that actively thinking of reasons is probably not the best way forward. Such an approach is simply too cognitive (a habitual error). Less thinking and more doing is a better way. If only I could actually do that.

–

Thursday 12 October

'You will not be punished for your anger; you will be punished by your anger.' This quote attributed to Buddha is annoyingly trite and even more annoyingly true.

Reflecting on one's own anger is difficult at the time when one is angry. *Of course I'm 100 per cent right!* But reflecting back on anger we seem to fall into the opposite trap, arguing that our anger was 100 per cent wrong. Both extremes are misleading. Anger often arises for an excellent reason: unfairness, injustice, random bad luck. It is mostly understandable at the time. How we deal with it is often less than optimal, but we also err when we denigrate ourselves too much in retrospect.

Humans are impulsive by nature, but when the heat has died down, we can learn if we reflect with calmness. We can learn if we just sit.

–

Friday 13 October

Very busy day at work: presenting at Grand Rounds in the hospital, participating in examinations all morning, seeing patients in the afternoon, catching up with emails, letters and phone calls until after 7. And then home.

It is difficult to find time to meditate on a day like today, but that probably just makes meditation even more important. Most emails require just a quick glance before deleting them, but a small number need some kind of response: filling in a form, scanning and emailing something or looking for information to respond to a query. I try to deal with all of the day's emails on the same day so as to carry none over to the following day, but this does not always work out. I should probably see emails as a flow that I dip into whenever I can rather than as an accumulation of tasks, each of which must be attended to.

I need to let more emails just float past, like intrusive thoughts during a meditation sit. That would be more Buddhist of me, I think.

–

Saturday 14 October

An evening at the theatre. We see Eugene McCabe's *King of the Castle* at the Gaiety. The story centres on a wealthy landowner and his young wife. They are unhappy. The play is relentlessly dark and, I find, entirely uninvolving. Perhaps I can't identify with the characters? Perhaps I'm just not in the right mood. Perhaps I'll never know.

Afterwards, we have cookies, which I enjoy greatly.

–

Sunday 15 October

I meditate today and think about more possible titles for this journal: *Confessions of a Zen Failure? The Scowling Monk and the Happy Lobster?* If the latter makes no sense, see the journal entry for Monday 21 August. I remain undecided.

–

Monday 16 October

Ireland braces for Hurricane Ophelia, the most extreme weather event in Ireland since 1961. In fact Ophelia has just been downgraded to a 'post-tropical cyclone' but it still has hurricane-force winds and can wreak havoc. The power of nature is truly awesome. In an era of astonishing technology and endless scientific advancement, with man impacting ever more on the rhythms of nature, nature still holds the ultimate power to humble us all. There is something majestic and dreadful about this kind of event: the terrible forces of nature slamming headfirst into the fragile civilisations of man. Albert Einstein: 'Look deep into nature, and then you will understand everything better.' This is a humbling day.

—

Tuesday 17 October

Self-immolation remains uncommon in the West. On 2 November 1965, however, an American Quaker named Norman Morrison set fire to himself outside the Pentagon to protest against the war in Vietnam. Intriguingly, Morrison, a family-oriented and peace-loving man, brought his baby daughter Emily to Washington DC with him on that day, but set her down safely some distance away before setting himself alight. Emily was unharmed and later re-united with her mother. There was no evidence that Morrison ever intended to harm Emily, although her presence at the scene added drama, poignancy and even greater mystery to Morrison's act of self-sacrifice.

Some four decades after Morrison's death his widow Anne Morrison Welsh wrote an extraordinary memoir of her life titled *Held in the Light: Norman Morrison's Sacrifice for Peace and His Family's Journey of Healing*, this month's book in my year-long meditation project. In her book, Anne Morrison Welsh tries to understand her husband's act and discovers that his self-immolation had, perhaps, its greatest impact in Vietnam itself, where Morrison is widely celebrated. But there remains a significant core of mystery at the heart of Morrison's self-immolation. It is an inevitable tragedy that a wife lost her husband and children their father. And even if Morrison's self-sacrifice had significant impact in the US and, especially, Vietnam, as his daughter later remarked, 'It didn't stop the war.'

Wednesday 18 October

I sit with renewed focus. I'm having one of my episodic periods of thinking that this journal has gone astray, devoting too much time to passing ephemera – plays, movies, books, the cat – and not focusing sufficiently on the mechanics and experience of meditating. So today I just sit, seeking to focus gently on my breath, letting other thoughts subside and fade away. I am moderately successful, which makes today a good day. Tomorrow might be even better.

–

Thursday 19 October

Time for some more Buddha quotes to lift the spirit: 'Irrigators channel waters; fletchers straighten arrows; carpenters bend wood; the wise master themselves.' Yes, but all of these tasks are highly, highly skilled. They are complex and difficult to teach. One can practise and accumulate the requisite skills over time, presumably: 'Drop by drop is the water pot filled. Likewise, the wise man, gathering it little by little, fills himself with good.'

–

Friday 20 October

The end of a working week and the start of the weekend. I wonder how are other meditators getting on out there? I am a solitary operator. Buddhists speak of the importance of community, or '*sangha*'. *Sangha* is one of the three 'jewels' of Buddhism; the others are the Buddha himself and the *dharma* (the teachings of the Buddha and the truth he understood). The *sangha* is the community of people with whom we practise and with whom we share our lives. According to the *Theravada* tradition within Buddhism, the *sangha* is characterised by 'practising the good way, practising the upright way, practising the knowledgeable or logical way, practising the proper way'. Surely, I need more *sangha*.

Saturday 21 October

I return to this month's theme, right effort, today, focused on keeping one's motivation and attitude positive, wholesome and directed towards Buddhist values, such as compassion, even if outcomes are initially disappointing. This is all a bit vague but it does seem important. Many things don't work out as we expect and the best intentions often go awry. That is presumably no reason to abandon our best intentions or abandon right effort. It is, rather, reason to pause, reflect and recalibrate, still in the context of right effort.

But does anyone consciously engage in wrong effort? I suppose we all act out of anger at times, as well as irritation, impatience, frustration and annoyance. We know we are doing so at the time – and yet we persist.

Presumably, some or all of this is avoidable if we make a conscious effort to keep our motivations and intentions clear in our heads and seek only to engage in acts that are 'skilful' in Buddhist terms. Operationalising right effort is, then, an essentially cognitive and emotional exercise, centred on keeping positive, ethical values central in our minds and ensuring that our behaviours reflect these values as best as possible.

–

Sunday 22 October

I'm trying hard today to operationalise right effort but I'm not certain I'm succeeding. At least I'm trying, I suppose. But does there ever come a point when trying is no longer enough and success becomes necessary? Is that point now? How would I know? These thoughts seem frustrating and circular and therefore non-productive. I set these questions to one side and go for a walk on a nice crisp evening: the trees are deep and wintery; the air is cold.

Monday 23 October

Work is busy today, the usual mix of assessing patients, talking with families, working with the team, responding to emails and letters and so forth. Each day comprises so, so many small actions: tens of thousands of tiny decisions and individual volitional actions that together make up the day. The day is like a sandstorm made up of countless grains of sand, each of which is unique (when you look closely enough) and all of which constitute an apparently unified phenomenon (when taken together and viewed as a whole). But appearances are illusory and the 'day' that I experience does not have a solid or fixed identity in and of itself. Like a murmuration of starlings, its essence is movement; it is built of change.

–

Tuesday 24 October

Buddha: 'Some do not understand that we must die, but those who do realise this settle their quarrels.' Buddhism accepts death as a fact of life. Buddhism's belief in reincarnation means that death provides opportunity for rebirth or, less literally, that the death of the 'old you' in your current life allows you to reinvent yourself. There can be many reincarnations in the course of a single human life. In every moment, we begin again.

–

Wednesday 25 October

And we're back to self-immolation. My return to this topic is prompted not only by the extent to which the act troubles me, but also the arrival of a book of reportage about Tibetan self-immolation, *Tibet on Fire: Self-Immolations Against Chinese Rule* by Tsering Woeser. I bought this volume when it appeared in French in 2013, titled *Immolations au Tibet: La Honte du Monde*. But my French let me down badly and I struggled to understand much of it at the time.

This new edition is fascinating and compelling. At the time of writing, 146 Tibetans had self-immolated and Woeser's book tries to contextualise and explain these acts. The brevity of the volume is no indicator of the impact of its contents. Woeser's account is movingly detailed, impassioned in its analysis and unsparing in its depiction of self-immolation. Woeser is alert to both the complexity and the tragedy of these acts, as well as the sense of injustice that fuels such extreme behaviour.

How desperate must you be to regard self-burning as the most eloquent way to express your distress?

–

Thursday 26 October

I meditate although I am still troubled by yesterday's reflections, at least initially. In time, I manage to let the troubling thoughts move past me and focus on my breathing. Again, there are birds singing outside, cars passing the front window and the mysterious sounds of floor-boards creaking through the house (even though there's no one else here). Sitting to meditate heightens awareness of all these things. You can experience a sort of hyper-reality which taunts you into noticing things you have never noticed before until you actively start trying not to notice them. Time to breathe and refocus again.

–

Friday 27 October

I browse multiple websites offering to email me daily messages about meditation. These are mostly free services offering prompts to medi-tate, positive messages about the benefits of contemplation, little gems of Buddhist wisdom, quotations from the Dalai Lama, etc. I have never signed up to any of these. My thinking is that I already receive a suffi-cient number of emails, messages and all kinds of communications each day. I need to just sit. And, today, I do.

Saturday 28 October

I meditate for twenty minutes with some degree of concentration. The time passes quickly now. I feel more settled, but still I do not levitate.

I read some Freud today as part of my annual reading of one of Freud's works. I've written about this project earlier this year and I include an essay about Freud, Beckett and various other matters after this month's journal entries, titled 'Ego, id and Ireland'.

Reading Freud today reminds me again of my fondness for projects: reading one volume of Freud per year, meditating for 20 minutes per day, and so forth. I enjoy both the specific acts (reading, meditating) but also the sense that they are part of a bigger picture. And the pattern suits me: moving along in slow, steady increments over a sustained period of time. There are 24 volumes of Freud, so that is an especially protracted undertaking. Who knows how long my meditation project will last? I'm hoping to keep going until the end of the year, but maybe I'll persist beyond then?

–

Sunday 29 October

I am approaching the end of the tenth month in my year-long meditation project. As usual I am full of doubts about the merits of the project and whether or not I've tried hard enough to date. The project has certainly increased my focus and concentration, and my awareness of my mental states, and I have spent a great deal of time thinking about the purpose of meditation, trying to meditate and reflecting on my successes and failures. To that extent at least, the project has worked out well. Of course, it could have been better: there's *duhkha* everywhere, so no conditioned phenomena are ever entirely satisfactory. But there is so much that has been positive over the past ten months that I am still firmly happy I undertook the project.

Monday 30 October

Perhaps this journal is the aspect of my project that has surprised me the most. I have never previously succeeded in keeping a journal of any description for any appreciable period of time. This time is different, possibly because this journal has a clear focus: meditation. And also, possibly, because I decided to write this journal as a time-limited project, with a clear beginning and end, and with a sense of purpose.

I have never been tempted to abandon the journal, even when I missed a couple of days and had to catch up later. And I think the journal has added significantly to my meditation project: it deepens and contextualises my efforts to meditate far more than it distracts me from them. But who knows if anyone will ever read it?

Tuesday 31 October

And, so my tenth month of daily meditation comes to an end. I sit for twenty minutes and then ponder the project to date. Less thinking and more meditating would still suit me better! But today is a good day, just like all the final days of the preceding nine months.

I have stuck with the project and have, I feel, earned some cake.

Conveniently, there is lemon drizzle cake to hand. It is not especially lemony but it is definitely cake. I eat it.

» *Ego, Id and Ireland*

The young man at the ticket office in the Freud Museum in Vienna is wearing fluorescent red sneakers. Out back, a woman dressed entirely in black stands on the fire escape, smoking in the European way: studied, unhurried. Sigmund Freud, the father of psychoanalysis, lived and worked here at Berggasse 19 in Vienna's ninth district from 1891 until his escape from the Nazis to London in 1938. Freud smoked too, and that was his downfall. In the 1920s the great man developed mouth cancer and, after a series of painful, arguably unnecessary operations, died in September 1939.

I have come to Vienna with my endlessly patient wife to pay homage to Freud for three reasons of varying validity. First, as a psychiatrist, the shadow of Freud inevitably looms large in my life. Today it often seems that novelists and artists find more value in Freud's work than psychiatrists do. But that is because Freud's insights are so embedded in our lives that we no longer attribute them to him. Freud created the language we use to think and talk about our minds. The fact that we think about our inner lives at all is largely attributable to Freud.

Second, I am Irish, and Freud is commonly quoted as saying that the Irish are the only people impervious to psychoanalysis. This was famously repeated in Martin Scorsese's 2006 film *The Departed*, prompting numerous journalists to search for comments from Irish psychiatrists: are the Irish really impenetrable to analysis?

Freud's statement played in my mind repeatedly over the past three years as I researched my book *Hearing Voices: The History of Psychiatry in Ireland*, which was published in November 2016 (to the immense relief of my long-suffering wife). Psychoanalysis is conspicuous by its absence in the history of psychiatry in Ireland, possibly owing to the Roman Catholic Church's opposition to it, the failure of Irish doctors to show the slightest interest at the time, or Ireland's position as an island, somewhat cut off from continental Europe.

The role of the Church is especially interesting. In Ireland, the Roman Catholic Church was deeply involved in politics, education, orphanages, and general health care, and it single-handedly dominated many areas of Irish life for much of the 1800s and 1900s. Even so, the Church did not develop formal, systematic involvement in mental health care. Why?

The reasons for this likely relate to the Church's attention to other areas such as schools and medical care, and the prominent involvement of figures from other religious traditions in early mental health care, most notably Jonathan Swift, an ordained priest in the Established Church of Ireland, who bequeathed his entire estate to establish the hospital for 'idiots and lunaticks' that later became St Patrick's Hospital, the first formal asylum in Ireland. Swift anticipated his own death:

He gave the little Wealth he had
To build a Home for Fools and Mad
And shew'd by one satyric Touch
No Nation wanted it so much.

While it is likely that certain people with psychological problems sought individual guidance from Roman Catholic priests or other religions, the Roman Catholic Church itself did not become systematically involved in formal mental health care in Ireland, with the result that the Irish asylums of the 1800s and 1900s were very much state institutions rather than Church ones.

Psychoanalysis, however, was the one area where the Church took a very public stand: it opposed Freudianism robustly. In 1963 the Archbishop of Dublin and Primate of Ireland, the Most Reverend John C. McQuaid, arguably the single most powerful figure in Irish public life, wrote an introduction to a remarkable, generally progressive book titled *The Priest and Mental Health*, in which McQuaid stated that Freud had not discovered reality but attempted to construct it. This was clearly intolerable to the Church. In that year, the Irish Psycho-Analytical Association (established in 1942) had just five practising psychoanalyst members and the Church seemed determined to keep it that way, ensuring that psychoanalysis, like communism, gained no significant foothold in Ireland.

There is, however, an intellectually lazy tendency to routinely blame the Church for everything that is regrettable or shameful in Irish history. This approach is certainly not without basis: the Church grossly betrayed the trust of many. But constructing the Church as an unremittingly evil 'other' also functions as a defence mechanism against broader societal complicity in various social problems and their so-called solutions, chiefly related to inappropriate institutionalisation and our historically harsh treatment of the disadvantaged. While the Church is indeed largely responsible for many of the ills of Irish history, blaming the Church automatically or entirely is at best reductive and at worst just plain wrong.

And maybe, of course, in addition to the Church's opposition to psychoanalysis, Freud was actually correct, and maybe the Irish really are impervious to his analytic technique. Maybe that is the real reason why psychoanalysis never really penetrated in Ireland. The only problem is that there's no evidence Freud ever made this remark. It appears to be a myth that emerged from nowhere, gained currency on the internet and is now liberally quoted. Its ubiquity is linked to the idea of the 'mad Irish', which suggests that the Irish are more prone to mental illness than other people – just as Swift mischievously hinted before his death.

But that, too, is a myth: the Irish do not have a higher rate of mental illness than anyone else, and never had. While we had more mental hospital beds per head of population than any other country in the mid 1900s, this was due to an epidemic of asylums rather than an epidemic of mental illness. We mixed bad laws with poverty and a fatal weakness for institutions, resulting in mass institutionalisation. It seems unlikely that any of this was due to a lack of psychoanalysis, which co-existed with enormous asylums in the US (Freudianism scarcely equated with freedom and might, in fact, be its opposite), but I suppose one never really knows. And regardless of whether or not he made the disputed statement, perhaps Freud did believe the Irish were impervious to psychoanalysis, and perhaps he was right, and perhaps that is where all the trouble started.

None of this, interestingly, stopped self-exiled Irish writers dipping into the rich well of psychoanalytic theory in their lives and work. Perhaps the Church's opposition actually encouraged them. Most famously, James Joyce brought his troubled daughter Lucia to Carl Jung in Switzerland for psychoanalysis. Jung's treatment programme focused on writing, interpretation of dreams and analysis of different kinds of transference. While Lucia's precise diagnosis varied between doctors, with some pointing towards psychosis and others towards neurosis, she appears to have had schizophrenia. This was, essentially, Jung's conclusion too: while he felt that Lucia's father was a genius, he believed Lucia was mentally ill. Both father and daughter had entered a river, but James was diving, Lucia falling.

In fact, Lucia was drowning. She was repeatedly hospitalised. In 1962, Irish writer Samuel Beckett donated his share of the royalties from a 1929 essay he wrote about Joyce's *Finnegans Wake* to help pay her hospital bills. Beckett, like Joyce, had an interest in psychoanalysis and, in 1933, commenced two years' treatment with psychoanalyst Wilfred Bion at London's Tavistock Clinic. Subtle psychoanalytic themes permeate Beckett's work, as do overtly psychiatric ones: part of his 1951 novel *Malone Dies* is set in a psychiatric hospital. Most of all, though, Beckett's writings present a vital and very Irish counterpoint to psychoanalysis: while both Beckett and the analysts plunge headlong into the psyche, Beckett's chiselled, searing prose contrasts with both

Freud's pedantry and Jung's psychedelia, and offers a literate, working philosophy of mind that vastly surpasses both.

So where does all of this get us? Despite high rates of psychiatric admissions, the Irish never had a higher rate of mental illness than any other people. The absence of psychoanalysis in Ireland is certainly linked with the Church's opposition to it, but other factors were also relevant, including a lack of medical interest and Ireland's precarious perch on the edge of Europe. Even so, Irish writers, including Joyce and Beckett, showed no hesitation in engaging with psychoanalysis, often quite profoundly. And finally, regardless of whether or not Freud said that the Irish are impervious to psychoanalysis, there is no particular reason to imagine that Irish life is any the worse for a lack of psychoanalysis, although most cultures would likely benefit from greater exposure to Freud himself who, despite his occasionally pedestrian prose, shone a light into areas of human life that rarely receive the attention they merit, even today.

All of which brings me to the third reason why I dragged my astonishingly tolerant, much put-upon wife to a chilly Vienna last November: eight years ago, for reasons that remain obscure even to me, I decided to read all twenty-four volumes of the *Standard Edition of the Complete Psychological Works of Sigmund Freud* at the rate of one volume per year. I write an essay each year in the *Irish Medical Times*. And I am currently reading (and enjoying) *Jokes and their Relation to the Unconscious*. It is funny. And while I am not exactly searching for Freud's quote about the Irish, I am keeping my eye out for it. There's no sign of it yet, but I'll let you know if it appears.

We exit the Vienna Freud Museum through the gift shop. I buy a Freud key ring, a Freud umbrella and two Freud frisbees for my children. We visit Café Landtmann, Freud's favourite café, where we eat Sachertorte, a chocolatey Viennese delight.

The ebullient waiter tells us in perfect English that the entire café is now a no-smoking zone. We are delighted although we imagine the master would not be pleased. The cake is delicious.

November

—

RIGHT MINDFULNESS

In which I continue to meditate and reflect on 'right mindfulness', the seventh element of the noble eightfold path of Buddhism and this month's theme in my year of daily meditation. I do my best to 'put aside worldly desire and sadness' but discover this is exactly as difficult as it sounds, if not more so. Undeterred, I continue my journey and read about Buddhist revivals and resurgences in India, Indonesia, Germany, the UK and the US, noting the intrinsic attractiveness of Buddhist philosophy and the deep hunger in many countries to look beyond local traditions in search of new meaning and new ways of seeing the world. Inevitably, other themes crop up over the course of the month: the nature of the working day, the meaning of the distractions that beset me from all angles, Buddha's ubiquitous words spreading across the internet and my continued lack of progress with meditation, despite a year of dedicated effort. I travel to Amsterdam and India, ending up in Delhi airport in the middle of the night, dislocated and disoriented but far from disenchanted. In summary: I keep going.

Wednesday 1 November

A new month. Buddha: 'The past is already gone; the future is not yet here. There's only one moment for you to live.' Now.

–

Thursday 2 November

I am very distracted today. There are a million things I could blame for this lamentable state of affairs: excessive work, poor sleep, hunger, irritation or simply the random events of the day. But those factors are always present to greater or lesser degrees, so it is difficult to know when one is simply using them as excuses and when one is truly confronted by too many obstacles at a given time.

The real problem lies with how I'm conceptualising the issue. Meditating well is not about meditating well; it is about trying to meditate well. That is meditation. That is right effort. That is the work of meditation. But it is difficult to keep this in mind and avoid becoming downhearted, especially on distracted, disjointed days like today. Still, this is what it's all about so I must simply carry on. Just that. Just sit.

–

Friday 3 November

Buddha: 'Radiate boundless love towards the entire world – above, below, and across – unhindered, without ill will, without enmity.' Boundless love. Who can achieve that?

I go for an evening walk on Poolbeg Pier. The water is pounding the pier ferociously. The sky is dark. There are few people here, just a couple of hardened dog walkers. And me. The water and the wind and the sky make me feel very, very small.

–

Saturday 4 November

This month's theme is 'right mindfulness', the seventh element of the noble eightfold path. Right mindfulness is topical at the moment. It is hard to avoid talk about mindfulness, in the media, in books, online, at work and even in casual conversations on the street. This is mostly good but it sometimes seems as if mindfulness is presented as the solution to everything. It is not.

I try to practise the 'mindfulness of breathing' today. But I am also mindful of the commodification and oversimplification of mindfulness. So, going back to the sources for this month's theme, what exactly is mindfulness according to Buddhist literature?

> *And what is right mindfulness? Here the monk remains contemplating the body as body, resolute, aware and mindful, having put aside worldly desire and sadness; he remains contemplating feelings as feelings; he remains contemplating mental states as mental states; he remains contemplating mental objects as mental objects, resolute, aware and mindful, having put aside worldly desire and sadness; this is called right mindfulness.*

–

Sunday 5 November

I think a little more about mindfulness, trying to contemplate 'mental states *as* mental states' (not as the be-all and end-all they sometimes feel like) and trying to remain 'resolute, aware and mindful' (as advised yesterday). There is, presumably, a thin line between being 'resolute' on the one hand and 'stubborn' on the other. Resolute sounds like a good thing whereas stubborn does not. Being resolute probably relates to focus and steadfastness rather than obstinacy and rigidity. I resolve to be resolute but not obstinate. I have no idea if I succeed but I stick with trying (resolutely? obstinately?).

Putting aside 'worldly desire and sadness' is difficult. 'Worldly desire and sadness' crop up every two minutes in the course of any given day and are incredibly difficult to 'put aside'. I imagine that mindfulness involves developing a greater sense of proportion about such emotions and judgements and ascribing the correct level of salience to the events of the day. It is easy to magnify a minor setback if one is already in a negative or irritated state of mind. The minute-to-minute ups and downs of life are so transitory, however, that it is idiotic to attach too much emotion to them, and yet we do it all the time. This is cognitively exhausting. Mindfulness seeks to increase awareness of this habit and diminish it.

–

Monday 6 November

Buddha speaks of the need for individual effort: 'You yourself must strive. The Buddhas only point the way.' Anger is one of the key obstacles to this kind of patient progress towards 'mastering' oneself: 'Whoever doesn't flare up at someone who's angry wins a battle hard to win.' Equanimity is the path *and* the destination.

–

Tuesday 7 November

It's the day of my annual 'diary changeover'. I still use a hand-held pocket diary that allows me to cross off tasks from the day's list as I do them. The fact that I use an old-style written diary also allows me to retain the mostly crossed-out list of tasks so that I can always check back later to see what I've done and what I haven't. I have yet to move on to using the electronic diary on my smartphone and I am not keen to do so. I depend on my phone for too many things already, and crossing things out in my pocket diary is a key part of how I work and organise my day. I am not my phone.

And so each year, at around this time, I transfer, by hand, all my future commitments and other diary entries to a brand new diary. My 2018 diary commences on 8 November 2017 so today is the big day this year. This evening I carefully copy all of my appointments and commitments for the coming year into my 2018 Hodges Figgis pocket diary. This is a useful exercise because I cancel or reschedule some of the appointments as I go through them in order to avoid overcommitment in early 2018. I end up with a clear picture of what lies ahead in the coming months.

I like my annual diary changeover. It is like spring cleaning. I always feel better after it. I certainly feel better after diary changeover than I usually feel immediately after meditating. Maybe this is what I should be aiming for after meditation: a feeling of cleansing and moving on? A refreshed sense of the future? Contentment? Happiness? Administrative tidiness? These are all good things.

–

Wednesday 8 November
I work all day and go to the book club in the evening. The book we discuss is *Conundrum* by Jan Morris.

Morris started life as 'James' (biologically male) but became 'Jan' (female) over the course of her life. She writes about her life with depth and colour, never short of an adjective or a well-turned phrase, always on the lookout for a telling anecdote or revealing fact. I enjoy her short book. Our discussion at the book club is considered and thoughtful, as the book club tends to be.

I wonder should I be increasing my meditation time. Aiming higher? Anyway, I do twenty minutes today in the midst of a busy but not unpleasant day. I especially enjoy the book club. It is one of life's understated pleasures.

–

Thursday 9 November
I attend a 'medical humanities' seminar at Trinity College Dublin. Medical humanities is an interdisciplinary field of research and practice that embraces medicine, the humanities, social sciences and the arts. Medical humanities explores these fields together, seeking areas of connection and interaction across traditional disciplinary boundaries. It is generally great fun and invariably thought-provoking.

I always enjoy events that link medicine with other disciplines: they open the mind and create space for reflection. I am increasingly taken with the value of reflectiveness, not just in terms of dedicating specific periods of time to contemplative practice (although that is clearly important) but also in terms of becoming a generally reflective person, routinely thinking carefully about things rather than simply lurching from one situation to the next, constantly in emergency mode.

Sometimes it's good to stop and think. To just sit.

—

Friday 10 November

I spend today in Belfast at meetings concerning Ireland's new Assisted Decision-Making (Capacity) Act 2015. This is an ambitious piece of legislation that seeks to better protect the autonomy of people with impaired mental capacity. I'm involved with the implementation process. Northern Ireland has new legislation too and today we discuss some joint research into specific aspects of legislative change across both jurisdictions.

All of this is by way of saying that I spend a lot of time on the train today. I have always found trains to be oddly contemplative spaces. Time spent on a train is protected from many of the distractions that beset us most other times. There are only so many things I can do on a train. Since I get travel sick if I read, I mostly listen to music or look out of the window. And every train journey has a specific, finite duration, which I am powerless to change: I cannot make the train go faster or slower. It's all very soothing and meditative.

—

Saturday 11 November

I sit briefly in the early morning and work until around 9 am. From that point on, the day is filled with family activities.

—

Sunday 12 November

Trixie is an exceptionally peculiar creature. She sits for impossibly long periods with minimal concern about what happens around her. She seeks out the busiest, noisiest part of the house and promptly falls asleep there. Some time later, she will suddenly dart across the room at high speed in a frenzy of excitement, only to stop abruptly and lick her leg. She will yawn, look around and fall sleep precisely where she is: in the middle of the floor, on the stairs, on a person. I wish I could sleep as she does: anywhere, anytime.

Today, when I should be meditating, I spend much time wondering what goes on in Trixie's head. Is her head cluttered with unwanted thoughts, just like mine?

She is a most companionable creature: sitting quietly by my computer as I type, stealing gently into the room as I sit. She has the gift of silence.

–

Monday 13 November

I return to this month's theme, right mindfulness. I do a quick Google search for 'mindfulness' and my laptop almost explodes: over 81 million webpages. I click through some of the top websites and, as usual, the content ranges from excellent, sensible meditation instructions to far-fetched theorising that makes no sense whatsoever. The internet is a truly awesome creation but its resources need to be used with keen critical awareness and a great deal of mindfulness. Indeed, if the internet has had any single effect on the human mind it is to increase the importance of critical thought: with infinite information at our fingertips, we need to sift it more carefully than ever.

Today's search yields all kinds of practical guidance about mindfulness, online tools, apps, books, courses, subscription offers, images, videos, e-books, retreat opportunities and even advice on how to use mindfulness to 'get rich'. In the end I set aside all the websites and try to focus on my breath. I have never found 'two-minute mindfulness' exercises helpful: my twenty minutes per day is necessary for me to achieve any kind of benefit from this practice.

So today I banish Google from my mind, sit for twenty minutes and try to focus on my breath. I do okay.

Tuesday 14 November

Buddha: 'A disciplined mind brings happiness.' Both discipline and happiness appear elusive. Are they the same thing? Does finding one mean finding the other?

I see patients as individual people, living their lives in the contexts of their families, communities and societies. But sometimes it's good to step back and look at the bigger picture – at population level. Globally, over 300 million people suffer from depression, the world's leading cause of disability. Each year, 800,000 people die by suicide, the second leading cause of death among 15–29 year olds. And despite these figures, the World Health Organisation reports that most of the people affected by mental illness – 75 per cent in many low-income countries – do not have access to the treatment they need. This is a humbling thought that plays on my mind today, for some reason.

In Ireland, hundreds of thousands of people attend GPs and various therapists for mental health problems each year; tens of thousands attend community mental health teams; and in 2017 there were almost 17,000 admissions to Irish psychiatric units and hospitals.

That's a lot of people. I reflect on the numbers for a while. For the second time this month, I feel very, very small.

–

Wednesday 15 November

More Buddha: 'It is in the nature of things that joy arises in a person free from remorse.' But how can one be truly 'free from remorse'? It must take constant effort and a great deal of willpower. Reading these online Buddha 'quotations' is slightly addictive but I'm not certain it's helpful. The odd quote here and there is vaguely inspirational but the inspiration passes quickly enough. *Duhkha* everywhere.

–

Thursday 16 November

I deliver two public lectures, attend a meeting about the mental capacity legislation, and see patients. It is a ridiculously busy day with diminished opportunity but increased need for contemplative time. I meditate for 20 rushed, unsatisfactory minutes. Sigh.

—

Friday 17 November

This month's book is *The World of Buddhism*, edited by Heinz Bechert and Richard Gombrich. I bought this book many years ago and it has served me well. This is slightly surprising because I commonly find multi-author books frustratingly unfocused. Too often they are oversized, overpriced and characterised by disjointed incoherence, as a random selection of topics receive idiosyncratic treatments at the hands of a variety of uninterested authors, selected for no apparent reason.

In fairness, not all multi-author volumes fit this paradigm and occasionally one will provide a good overview of key themes and leave the reader with a genuine desire to seek out more information about specific topics of interest. *The World of Buddhism* belongs firmly in the latter category.

What I love most about it are the images. Buddhism has a rich visual heritage, which serves as a useful antidote to the more cognitive aspects of practice.

—

Saturday 18 November

I wonder where my interest in Buddhism comes from. I've been dimly aware of Buddhism since I was a child but it only caught my imagination in a big way in my twenties. Religions interest me anyway, especially the way they produce extreme devotion in some people, quiet commitment in others and complete indifference in yet others. There can be no doubt that religious traditions evolve to meet human needs for meaning, for group belonging and for celebration or comfort at times of transition (birth, marriage, illness, death).

I find the core concepts of Buddhism instinctually attractive, especially the idea that one can control one's mind through meditative practice and thus understand things better, seeing reality as it truly is.

Sunday 19 November

I'm greatly enjoying a travel book titled *A Journey into Russia* by Jens Mühling. This interesting, peculiar book is centred on Mühling's exploration of Russia through the prism of specific cities and regions, which he couples with elemental forces: Kiev ('ice'), Moscow ('blood'), Saint Petersburg ('wind'), Siberia ('water'), the steppes ('grass') and taiga ('wood'). Mühling recounts his intrepid travels in Russia through a mixture of history, anecdote and reflective musing. Perhaps inevitably, much of his book deals with issues of religion as well as the political turmoil that characterises so much of Russia's past.

Anyone who has read my journal to this point will not be surprised when I say that I love Saint Petersburg. I visited over twenty years ago and I remember it vividly still: the majestic buildings, the Neva river, the mysteriousness of its side streets and its enormous, melancholic museums. I especially remember a smaller museum near the banks of the Neva, filled with curiosities and 'grotesqueries' of all descriptions: misshapen skeletons, specimens in jars, and bizarre bits and pieces from around the world.

I would love to travel more in Russia, just like Mühling. But, instead, today I meditate quietly, placing all thoughts of further Russian travel to one side for now.

–

Monday 20 November

I'm reading a lot more: more travel books, long magazine articles and even one or two novels. In the past I read a great deal of fiction but this declined over the years as work took over. But these past few months have seen my concentration and patience for other kinds of reading increase. This is gratifying: I had started to think that while I could concentrate endlessly on work or academic writing, my leisure time concentration was now limited to 25-minute sitcoms. Not so, it seems!

Tuesday 21 November

Rain. It starts gently, gathers power, and then lashes mercilessly against the car windows, my coat, my hat. I get soaked. I leave water dripping after me as I arrive to work. My coat takes all day to dry in the office and then gets wet again immediately as I leave to go home. The rain does not stop, but it provides a pleasing, rhythmic backdrop for my meditation sit later in the evening.

–

Wednesday 22 November

I return to this month's book, *The World of Buddhism*. The final chapter deals with the 'Buddhist revival in East and West' and captures my imagination because it deals with the beginnings of Western Buddhism, Buddhist modernism and Buddhist revivals or resurgences in India, Indonesia, Germany, the UK and the US.

Buddhism has travelled very well over the past century or two, and its ideas are now commonplace in media, publications and websites around the world. This is attributable to both the intrinsic attractiveness of Buddhist philosophy and a hunger to look beyond local traditions in search of new ways of seeing the world.

For many people Buddhism provides precisely this: a fresh way of looking at one's life and a new set of ideas about how to live better and be happier. Ironically, much Buddhist advice on these themes is already available within the native spiritual traditions of countries that have welcomed Buddhism. But that, too, is something that Buddhism teaches: the importance of seeing clearly what is already in front of you and what is already within you, keeping your vision free of distraction, distortion and (ideally) desire. Everything is right there in front of us, if only we could see it as it really is.

Thursday 23 November

More rain. The rain is both a distraction from and an aid to meditation. When I should be focused on my breathing, it is difficult not to think about how wet I got outside, whether my coat will dry quickly and where I need to go to next. Will I get wet again? But rain also teaches acceptance: we cannot control the rain, we can only control the extent to which we let it trouble our minds. And I've always liked sitting beside an open window when the rain is falling straight down – not coming in the window or wetting me, but falling past the window. At such moments, there is a freshness and immediacy about nature that is very Zen.

–

Friday 24 November

No rain. Today brings a succession of patients who present with such complex problems that the best response to many is for me to just sit (as it were) and let them tell their stories in full without any interruption whatsoever. Oftentimes that can be enough for a first visit, and it will take a second or third visit before we can focus on the first one or two aspects of the situation that appear most amenable to change. Today there are stories of childhood abuse, homelessness, drug misuse, family break-ups, suicidal thoughts, and anxiety so bad that one man can barely leave his home. I listen to all of this and make what suggestions I can. But there's a lot to take on board and I am happy that I manage to meditate fairly well later on. It really does settle me after the day.

–

Saturday 25 November

A man went to see a mystic in order to find out how to be freed from his attachments and cravings. On hearing the man's question, the mystic jumped up, ran to a pillar and stood with his arms wrapped tightly around it. The mystic shouted: 'Save me from this pillar! Save me from this pillar!' The man was disappointed that the mystic was behaving so bizarrely and did not seem able to answer his question. A small crowd gathered, looking at the mystic with his arms clasping the pillar. The man became angry and said to the mystic: 'I came to you with a question and you are unable to answer. You are holding the pillar. It is not holding you. You can just let go.' The mystic let go of the pillar at once and said to the man: 'If you understand that, you have your answer. The chains of attachment are not holding you. You are holding them.'

–

Sunday 26 November
I sit quietly for twenty surprisingly satisfactory minutes.

–

Monday 27 November
To Amsterdam. This is the first step in a ten-day work trip to the Netherlands and India, researching mental health law in India. India has just radically revised its mental health legislation with its Mental Healthcare Act 2017: given that India has a population of over 1.3 billion people, the new legislation is one of the most important pieces of mental health legislation on the planet. It is also one of the most progressive, at least in theory, because it grants a legally binding right to mental healthcare to one-sixth of the planet's population.

The legislation states that 'every person shall have a right to access mental healthcare and treatment from mental health services run or funded by the appropriate Government'. Government 'shall make sufficient provision as may be necessary for a range of services required by persons with mental illness'.

It is not yet clear how this ambitious undertaking will work out in practice. This level of commitment to promoting rights would present a challenge in almost any country and it is greatly encouraging to see such a large country taking this assertive step forward.

Tuesday 28 November

I love Amsterdam. It fits in squarely with my fondness for European cities: streets lined with old buildings, endless canals, trees and bicycles everywhere. We had good meetings yesterday afternoon and into the evening, discussing the new Indian legislation. I spend today working on it again until around 5.30 pm. Once finished, I head out and as I type these words I am sitting in a cake shop eating a ridiculously unhealthy chocolate truffle cake and drinking green tea. I've already visited the American Book Centre and wandered along a succession of canals.

Suddenly a pigeon flies into the café and goes under the table, pecking hopefully around my shoe. This pigeon has lost a foot but someone has given him a prosthetic foot that keeps him moving effectively. I throw him a fragment of chocolate truffle cake but he has no interest in it. Perhaps it's too unhealthy for him? Undeterred, he hops onto the table to investigate my green tea.

–

Wednesday 29 November

We leave Amsterdam around midday. I wake up early and work for a couple of quiet hours before going to the airport. It's a busy day, filled with hustle and hurry, packing up and moving on.

But travel actually helps me to meditate, overall. While there is bustle and distraction during the journey itself, there is also discovery and the glorious sense of being somewhere that is foreign to the everyday. Hotels are helpful as they place limits on distraction and provide quietude for meditation. And then there is the delightful contrast between the clamour of an airport and the solitude that travel can bring: being alone in a place where absolutely no one knows you is liberating and intoxicating and highly conducive to change. India!

–

Thursday 30 November

We arrive in Delhi airport in the early morning and wait ten hours for an internal Indian flight. As I sit, dazed and confused, I realise that

this is the final day of the penultimate month in my year-long meditation project. Eleven months done; one to go. What have I learned, if
anything?

As before, I am taken with the paradox that it remains challenging
to make time for meditation but it is always richly rewarding when I do.
Why is there still such behavioural resistance to a practice that is clearly
helpful and positive?

On 31 January I wrote that 'it takes at least three months to establish
a new habit'. Ten months later I have sustained a modest meditation
practice, but has it become a firm habit? Or are my efforts still 'uneven,
overambitious and fairly random'? I'm pretty sure I've made progress
but there is still more unevenness and randomness than I would like. I
must keep going. I must keep on keeping on.

But for now, stranded in Delhi airport in the middle of the night, I
search for cake. I find none.

December

—

RIGHT CONCENTRATION

In which my year of daily meditation draws to a close
with a by-now familiar mix of meditation, reflection
and distraction (especially distraction). I travel around
northern India and visit Bodhgaya, where Buddha is said
to have attained enlightenment. Bodhgaya is a wonderful
place, filled with pilgrims and chaos and life and animals
and dust (especially dust). I reflect on this month's theme,
'right concentration', and revisit a favourite Buddhist
introductory text as this month's book. I also reflect on
the rights of the mentally ill, my tendency to concentrate
fiercely on inconsequential matters and the reported
usefulness (for some) of Buddhist concepts in the process
of diagnosing mental illness. Other themes appear along
the way: traffic, cows, trees, Christmas lights, vegetarianism, more cows, more trees, happiness, various philosophers and, of course, Trixie the cat, who is the chief,
persisting enigma throughout this journal.

Friday 1 December

I have an auspicious start to the new month: I spend the day in Bodh-gaya, a pilgrimage town with a population of around 45,000 in the Indian state of Bihar. Bodhgaya is where Buddha is said to have attained enlightenment, so it is a key stopping point on this trip and in this journal.

As I've previously recounted, the young Buddha, known as Siddhārtha, was dissatisfied with his early life of privilege and become a wandering ascetic or *śramana*. After several years of meditation and self-mortification, he remained unfulfilled and went to meditate under a sacred bodhi tree, vowing that he would die beneath the tree rather than arise without wisdom. Despite various challenges, Siddhārtha duly attained enlightenment during a night of meditation and finally saw the exact condition of all living beings and the cause of and solution to suffering. At this point, Siddhārtha became a 'Buddha' or awakened one.

The bodhi tree beneath which Buddha sat is said to be located in Bodhgaya. Today, I sit below that very tree – recognisable by its heart-shaped leaves – in the Mahabodhi Temple Complex in Bodhgaya and try very, very hard to become enlightened. I'm pretty sure that's not how enlightenment works, but I have a go anyway.

Bodhgaya is an inspiring place filled with tourists and pilgrims, noise and quietness, desperation and joy, hope and miracles. There are cows, dogs, camels and birds in cages, which you pay to release ('good karma').

There are people everywhere. And dust. Lots and lots of dust. Vendors line the streets selling Buddha statues of all shapes and sizes for travellers of all shapes and sizes: the dreamers, the seekers and the spiritual tourists who flock here in their millions. And me: I buy some Buddha statues, Buddha stickers, Buddha bangles and two balloons which, when inflated, will be very large indeed. The balloons are not Buddha-shaped (thankfully), but pretty much everything else here is.

I like Bodhgaya a lot.

Saturday 2 December

Of all the unlikely places for me to end up, I travel today to Patna, a city of approximately two million people in north-eastern India. The capital of the state of Bihar, Patna has a long history as a centre for learning and fine arts, home to astrologists and scholars. I am here to meet with Indian psychiatrists, organise focus groups, plan future collaborations and deliver some lectures and talks.

I love India. I have always wanted to travel everywhere and, even as a child, I found the idea of Asia especially appealing. I later enjoyed trips to Japan and China and last year visited India for the first time. I spent a week in Bangalore and was utterly entranced by the bustle, the intensity and the feel of the streets: deeply unfamiliar and strangely intoxicating.

I think part of me just loves any country that is profoundly different to my home country. I love the way that other countries look, smell, taste, sound and feel so different to home. India does all of these things and more.

Patna delivers in spades: walking its streets, I might as well be in a dream.

–

Sunday 3 December

My colleague and I talk today with Indian psychiatrists about the human rights implications of India's new Mental Healthcare Act 2017. Properly implemented, legislation such as this plays a key role in protecting the rights of the mentally ill, ensuring access to care, and increasing social justice for the mentally ill, their families and carers.

This development, however, also presents real and urgent challenges to mental health legislators and service providers, especially in connection with involuntary care, people who lack mental capacity, and substitute decision-making. Nevertheless, the strong incentive for reform and the impetus for change reflected in the Indian Act is an opportunity that should not be missed. The legislation offers much that is positive and progressive in terms of standards of care, new procedures for involuntary admission, *de facto* decriminalisation of suicide and enhanced governance. It is also important that such initiatives focus not only on the right to liberty but also on rights to treatment, social care, social inclusion and political empowerment of the mentally ill.

These are big, important issues. After today's animated and positive discussions I sit somewhat wearily before bed. Sleep!

–

Monday 4 December

We fly from Patna to Ranchi, capital of the Indian state of Jharkhand, over 300 kilometres away. Ranchi is the second Indian city in which we are scheduled to meet with Indian psychiatrists. Goodness: another bustling Indian city, this time with a population of 1.1 million. There are so many big, bustling cities in India! Time and again I am struck by just how large this country is. The territory is vast; there are people *everywhere*; and the population is still growing.

That said, Ranchi is substantially smaller than, say, Bangalore. I am struck by the thought that most of my travels, both in India and elsewhere, take me to cities rather than rural areas. I wonder is this a modern thing? I know that, globally, cities are growing rapidly all the time: the World Health Organisation points out that, in 2014, the planet's urban population accounted for 54 per cent of the total, up from 34 per cent in 1960, and is continuing to grow. Urban population growth is concentrated in the less developed regions of the world and soon a majority of people will be living in urban areas, even in less developed countries.

I think about this today in Ranchi as we get settled in and plan our three-night stay: more meetings, discussions, focus groups and lectures. I like this kind of thing. I sit for twenty minutes in reflective mood.

Tuesday 5 December

The traffic in India is really crazy. Cars, buses, trucks, tuk-tuks (auto-rickshaws or 'autos'), bicycles, motorbikes, cows, dogs, camels and of course people all use the road for many different purposes, all at the same time. Tiny children race out between cars. Men wash their teeth on the road, ambling between whizzing vehicles. Groups of women sail across the street in dazzling saris, untroubled by the swirling dust and traffic thundering around them.

And then there are the cows. Mostly scrawny and unkempt, the sacred cows drift about the place utterly unfazed by the traffic, the continuous honking of car horns and the general chaos. But it's not real chaos, of course: a traffic intersection in India is an intricate feat of mutual adjustment and interaction, as dozens of people alter their trajectories and speeds very, very subtly based on the trajectories and speeds of others, leaving just millimetres and milliseconds to spare between them. It should not work but, by and large, it does.

Gazing at a busy traffic intersection here is terrifying and breathtaking and amazing. It is also oddly meditative; there is a calming quality to such condensed interaction that is unexpectedly disarming and not at all unpleasant. I will miss it when I return home – but I would never, ever drive here.

–

Wednesday 6 December

We hold focus groups at the Central Institute of Psychiatry in Ranchi and I give a lecture about ethics and mental health legislation. It all goes well.

I both struggle with and enjoy Indian food. I'm anxious about food poisoning so I'm cautious about what I eat. I stick to cooked food and, without explicitly deciding to, have gone vegetarian for the week. This is no problem: the Indian food is so spicy that every dish is incredibly delicious to me. I have an odd sense of taste that leads me firmly towards spicy dishes. The stand-out event of this trip so far has been the sweet chilli potato I had in Patna three days ago. It is worth travelling to India for that alone.

Perhaps this trip will finally move me towards a more vegetarian diet and away from the reliance on burgers that I have lamented at various points throughout this journal. One should not kill and eat sentient beings, and yet one does.

—

Thursday 7 December

And so our Indian trip comes to an end. We leave Ranchi this morning and head to the airport. Much as I like India, this has been a work trip. My colleague and I have spent most of our time travelling, attending meetings, holding focus groups, participating in teaching sessions and writing papers into the night. I'm utterly exhausted. I've meditated but not especially well.

It is coming near Christmas but there is no sign of it here at Ranchi airport. I'm sure Dublin is awash with lights, shoppers and pre-Christmas bustle. We fly from Ranchi to Delhi and from there to Amsterdam. More airports, more flights, more time spent trying to connect with dodgy wifi. The word that comes to mind is *saṃsāra*, the Sanskrit term for cyclic change that never ends, the constant, repetitive churning of life, like a hamster on a treadmill. I try to see if inflight movies can break the cycle of *saṃsāra* on this journey but the Buddhists are probably correct: only true enlightenment can free me. For the moment, I stick with second-rate inflight movies and try (but fail) to sleep.

—

Friday 8 December

Jet-lagged, disoriented and a little dehydrated, I arrive back in Dublin from Amsterdam. Thank goodness it's Friday! I have the weekend to recover and reorganise after my travels. Everywhere is full of seasonal cheer and tinsel. There's plenty of genuine joy as reunions occur all around me in the airport, even if this joy is mixed with the grim, relentless commercialisation of Christmas grinding along in the background. So be it. It's good to be home. Later, the jet-lag neither hinders nor aids my meditation. It is oddly irrelevant. That is a good sign, I think.

Saturday 9 December

This month's theme in my meditation project is 'right concentration', the eighth and final element in Buddhism's noble eightfold path. In a sense, this entire year has been about cultivating right concentration: seeking to expand and deepen meditative practice, enhance focus and increase clarity of thought. This has been a partial success with, perhaps, greater progress in establishing a meditation habit than in other areas of spiritual endeavour.

But I suppose one must not rush and there is much to be said for prioritising cultivation of right concentration in the first instance. Other developments will follow, perhaps. Establishing the *behaviour* of meditating is surely a key first step, an important, scene-setting, behavioural and cognitive shift.

But what, precisely, is right concentration? There is much guidance available on this topic, mostly centred on attaining mindfulness and focus while also overcoming anxiety and restlessness. These are key meditative skills that sound simple in theory but require great discipline in practice: while mindfulness is commonly associated with relaxation, it is equally associated with alertness or, more precisely, *awareness*, making its attainment a complex balancing act.

In this context, right concentration means removing focus from the non-essential in order to focus better on the essential: assigning salience correctly; and deepening one's awareness of what is important, real and true.

–

Sunday 10 December

Not much right concentration today, I'm afraid. But I meditate on, fixedly. I'm still re-adjusting to Ireland after my trip and remain a little unsettled.

This evening we go to Dublin Zoo to see 'Wild Lights', an incredible display of lanterns, which includes a pride of lions, orangutans, tigers, giraffes, monkeys and various other animals. It is very atmospheric and appropriate to a chilly evening in the pre-Christmas period. There is a 16-metre-high porcelain elephant tower, a 30-metre-long Chinese dragon, a Chinese craft market, Chinese performers and plenty of Chinese food.

I like this kind of thing. I have an attraction to Asian culture and cherish happy memories of a trip to China several years ago. Our evening at the lanterns in Dublin Zoo is most enjoyable and sufficiently Christmassy to reorient me back to life in Ireland after my Indian adventures.

–

Monday 11 December
Today I just sit. This meditation practice avoids many of the more cognitive and emotional exercises that often feature in meditation, such as counting breaths, cultivating loving kindness and so forth. It is a good exercise that really tests one's focus and ability simply to sit there meditatively. For me, this practice usually highlights just how full of chatter and clutter and clatter my mind is. But after around ten minutes of just sitting, the pointless babble in my head diminishes and things quieten down. I'm not certain that I ever really *just* sit but it's a good, humbling exercise.

–

Tuesday 12 December
Buddha: 'Know from the rivers in clefts and in crevices: those in small channels flow noisily, the great flow silent. Whatever's not full makes noise. Whatever is full is quiet.'

–

Wednesday 13 December
I am still thinking about yesterday's quote, that 'whatever is full is quiet'. Perhaps I should stay quiet today.

Thursday 14 December

As the years go by I become fonder and fonder of trees. Trees are splendid (and quiet). Rabindranath Tagore: 'Trees are the earth's endless effort to speak to the listening heaven.'

–

Friday 15 December

I return to this month's theme, right concentration. I often find myself concentrating quite fiercely on various minor tasks, such as achieving a small aim like travelling from A to B during the working day. I sometimes alarm myself at how concentrated I become on these relatively minor tasks, grossly out of proportion with their importance. It is easy to get swept up in the thousands of small events and tasks that constitute daily life. Emails are especially pernicious.

But all of these small events and tasks *are* important: they are how we live and communicate with each other, how we move through the world, how we work, how we play and how we define ourselves. Buddhism teaches that the 'self' that seems to be doing all these things is an illusory concept. The self is constantly changing in response to external circumstances and therefore lacks sustained identity or firmness. Everything is in a state of flux, so efforts to micromanage our environments, reflected in the fierce concentration we bring to minor daily tasks, are profoundly futile.

That is not to say that we are without agency or power, or that we should not concentrate on what we do. Quite the opposite. We have considerable agency to decide what we do and what we concentrate on. And we should use that agency better, to assign salience to what is important and let other things slip past. Awareness is key: awareness of what we are thinking and feeling, awareness of the world around us and awareness of the deep, deep impermanence that lies at the heart of all perceived phenomena.

I make a brief appearance on *The Late Late Show* this evening, talking about suicide. The show is unspeakably moving and this difficult theme is handled very well by the guests, the producers and Ryan Tubridy.

Saturday 16 December

Not too much right concentration today but I have plenty of awareness of my lack of concentration. Is that progress? Perhaps it's a first step towards achieving better concentration and better control of my mind. And that, Buddhism teaches, does not just lead to happiness; that *is* happiness. Happiness *is* the path and is achievable, it seems, with 'right concentration'.

All the great philosophers agree. Confucius: 'The more man meditates upon good thoughts, the better will be his world and the world at large.' Aristotle: 'Happiness depends upon ourselves.' Mencius: 'The myriad things are complete in us. There is no greater joy than to reflect on ourselves and become sincere.' Plato: 'The man who makes everything that leads to happiness depends upon himself, not upon other men, and has adopted the best plan for living happily.' Lao Tzu: 'If you are depressed you are living in the past. If you are anxious you are living in the future. If you are at peace you are living in the present.'

But one can try too hard. Thoreau: 'Happiness is like a butterfly: the more you chase it, the more it will elude you, but if you turn your attention to other things, it will come and sit softly on your shoulder.'

–

Sunday 17 December

I think back to my India trip, especially Bodhgaya and the thousands of pilgrims. There were many different kinds of Buddhist monks and nuns, dressed in a variety of ways. Some were chanting rhythmically and paying homage to Buddha. Others were meditating in silence. Some were reciting prayers from well-worn prayer books and pieces of parchment. Others repeatedly prostrated themselves beneath the branches of the bodhi tree. Buddha attained enlightenment there. I wonder did they?

Equally interesting were the guests at our hotel, mostly tour groups from Japan, dressed entirely in white. Many Japanese people visit Bodhgaya each year, it seems. The ones we met were in large groups but were unfailingly quiet and subdued, in stark contrast to the noise and bustle of the Indian streets. But most of all I remember the town of Bodhgaya itself, its streets lined with vendors, people thronging to the temple to see the tree, and dust and life in abundance all around.

–

Monday 18 December

Buddha: 'Three things cannot be long hidden: the sun, the moon, and the truth.' There are many variations on this quote but I like this one best: clear, simple, true.

–

Tuesday 19 December

When I meet people each day in my role as a psychiatrist, they invariably come with different forms of distress and unique combinations of problems. Everyone is different. This is what makes my job interesting, complex and a great privilege.

As a result of this diversity, there have been long-standing movements to standardise diagnosis in psychiatry, insofar as such a thing is possible. That is to say, there are ongoing efforts to define specific clinical conditions so that everyone who uses the term 'schizophrenia', for example, knows they are talking about roughly the same thing. This is especially important for those doing research into new treatments or reviewing the work of mental health professionals to ensure standards are being met.

Two main symptom-based classification systems have emerged: the *International Classification of Diseases* (ICD-10), with its 'Classification of Mental and Behavioural Disorders', published by the World Health Organisation (1992) and the *Diagnostic and Statistical Manual of Mental Disorders* (DSM-5) published by the American Psychiatric Association (2013). In both systems, specific diagnoses are defined by the presence of specific symptoms from specific lists for specific periods of time at specific levels of severity. Both diagnostic systems are imperfect and both are important.

There are, of course, quite profound contradictions and tensions inherent in the entire diagnostic enterprise. Isn't everyone different and unique? Isn't it hugely unlikely that anyone's particular psychological distress will map precisely onto pre-existing, one-fits-all categories made out by committees in different countries, all of whom keep changing the categories every few years anyway? Whose interest is really served by these elaborate diagnostic systems?

Much of this criticism relates to misuse of these systems rather than their correct use. Both diagnostic systems warn sternly against tick-box diagnosis, emphasising the importance of the person's own story and developing an understanding of their suffering. And many people derive significant benefit from diagnostic systems used in this flexible way, because they identify with certain features of clinical descriptions and feel reassured that other people have experienced something similar to what they are experiencing now. They are not alone.

It has been my view for some time that more skilful engagement can be facilitated for some people through concepts like 'dependent arising' and 'nonself', and specifically the idea that perceived phenomena (including the self) are entirely dependent on external causes and conditions for their apparent existence and are thus without fixed substance, permanence or truly independent existence. This casts the diagnostic process in quite a different light, making it humbler, gentler, and more geared towards mutual understanding.

Diagnosis is an important task. If it is done, it must be done with wisdom, humility and compassion. These are all key features of Buddhist philosophy.

—

Wednesday 20 December

More on psychiatric diagnosis today! The US diagnostic system, the *Diagnostic and Statistical Manual of Mental Disorders* (DSM-5), is often described as the 'Bible' for psychiatrists, but practice varies greatly. Some psychiatrists (chiefly in the US) consult DSM-5 commonly, others ignore it completely and a great majority draw on it selectively, focusing on parts that make sense to them and completely ignoring large sections that do not. So, just like the Bible.

Thursday 21 December

What can I say about Trixie? She sits contemplating me right now as I type this journal, staring, unblinking. I close my eyes. When I open them twenty minutes later, she is gone.

–

Friday 22 December

Molière: 'The trees that are slow to grow bear the best fruit.' Walt Whitman: 'Why are there trees I never walk under but large and melodious thoughts descend upon me?' 'Large and melodious thoughts' sound wonderful! How come I never have any? Maybe I don't walk under enough trees.

Today I hear that Richard, one of my long-standing patients with schizophrenia, died a couple of days ago, of cancer. One of the saddest things about the patients I see, especially those with enduring illnesses, is that they die so young: men with schizophrenia die fifteen years earlier, and women twelve years earlier, than the general population. The most common causes are heart disease and cancer, worsened by poor access to medical care. People with enduring mental illness are also at increased risk of unemployment, homelessness and imprisonment, even for minor offences. Richard experienced all of these.

While some of these problems relate to mental illnesses themselves, many relate more closely to the unforgiving social context in which mental illness occurs, a general lack of understanding and the persistent stigma wrongly associated with conditions such as depression, bipolar disorder, schizophrenia, personality disorders and so forth.

But, despite today's incredibly sad news, I know there are many reasons to be hopeful. Treatments for mental illness are just as effective as treatments in other areas of medicine, if not more so. And for the minority who need inpatient mental health care, Ireland has moved from a position where we had proportionally more people in psychiatric hospitals than any other country in the world in the 1950s to the position today, when our rate of involuntary care is less than half of that in England. While this reflects greater respect for the right to liberty, it is important that community services are continually enhanced so as to provide more comprehensive 24/7 support to those who need it.

This is important. One person in every four will develop a mental illness at some point in life. There is no 'them'; there is only 'us'.

I think about Richard a lot today.

–

Saturday 23 December

This month's book is one I have enjoyed for many years, guiding me clearly and directly though Buddhist thought and tradition. *The Foundations of Buddhism* by Rupert Gethin is gloriously easy to read, logical and insightful. Gethin outlines the story of the Buddha, explores the key teachings with remarkable clarity and concludes by discussing evolving Buddhist traditions in various places around the world.

I return repeatedly to this book. It is difficult to say why or how a particular book makes its way into one's mind and lodges there. There is, perhaps, a specific mix of information, tone of voice and balance between fact and interpretation that makes this volume memorable for me.

I should, perhaps, have mentioned this book at the start of this year; it is, after all, a superb introductory text. But rereading it now, toward the end of the year, highlights just how important an introductory text can continue to be, even long after the time for introductions has passed. Or maybe the time for introductions never really passes?

Outside my window: a squirrel.

–

Sunday 24 December

It is almost a cliché to say that Christmas is a difficult time for many people, but like many clichés this one is true. And this is something we do to ourselves. We place ourselves and each other under enormous pressure to socialise, meet with other people and enjoy ourselves in specific ways, whether or not we really wish to. Those who cannot or do not want to participate are seen as either peculiar or to be pitied. As a result, Christmas is a time when solitude is especially to be valued, particularly the psychological space that can be cleared through meditation.

–

Monday, 25 December

Christmas! The consumerism and gluttony of the Christmas season rest uneasily with Buddhism, but other aspects fit right in: appreciating other people, giving gifts (especially thoughtful, symbolic ones), and taking time out from the run of daily life to spend with other people. Over the years, I've seen many patients who dread Christmas as a time of loneliness and stress, and mental health services tend to be especially busy in the run-up to Christmas. But today I enjoy the day and even squeeze some meditation into the festive mix.

–

Tuesday 26 December

Paying attention, carefully and mindfully, is invariably rewarding. Buddha: 'Delight in heedfulness! Guard well your thoughts!' Discipline is paradoxically liberating: 'Just as the great ocean has one taste, the taste of salt, so also this teaching and discipline has one taste, the taste of liberation.' It is challenging: 'Just as treasures are uncovered from the earth, so virtue appears from good deeds, and wisdom appears from a pure and peaceful mind. To walk safely through the maze of human life, one needs the light of wisdom and the guidance of virtue.' To attain this, 'one must first discipline and control one's own mind. If a person can control their mind they can find the way to enlightenment, and all wisdom and virtue will naturally come to them.'

–

Wednesday 27 December

Back at work today, but it is still Christmas. I sit, celebrate and eat chocolate.

Thursday 28 December

Clinical work carries on continually over Christmas and New Year in the hospitals. We all chip in over the holiday season and if anyone takes leave it's only for short periods for specific, family reasons. We arrange to cover each other so that services operate all the time. The emergency department never closes and patients arrive at all hours of day and night. In psychiatry we see a lot of distress related to family arguments, alcohol and drug misuse, and people who struggle to cope with the pressure of the season. It's a busy time clinically and today, for me, there is plenty of clinical work but also, later, more Christmas, more chocolate and twenty minutes of meditation.

–

Friday 29 December

I'm looking at a wooden carving of Buddha that I bought at a street stall in Bodhgaya earlier this month. Buddha is in his ascetic phase: bearded, gaunt and thin. His ribcage is prominent through his chest wall. In this part of his story, Buddha's renunciation had a strong physical component: he fasted and engaged in lengthy periods of punishing, solitary, contemplative practice.

Renunciation in one's mind is probably just as difficult to achieve and sustain as bodily renunciation. I have not done much renouncing of any description during my year of daily meditation: going vegetarian for a week in India scarcely counts; it was a delight.

Still, I tried to meditate as best I could and, as end of year approaches, I reflect upon the past twelve months and wonder what it all might mean.

–

Saturday 30 December

I really admire trees. Dōgen Zenji, founder of the Sōtō school of Zen in Japan: 'Working with plants, trees, fences and walls, if they practise sincerely they will attain enlightenment.' Maybe that is what I need to do. Thoreau would approve. I should get more involved with trees.

Sunday 31 December

So, this is it: the end. I've meditated every day for a year. What have I to show for it? Is that even the right question to ask? Perhaps this isn't the end, only the beginning. Or the end of the beginning? Or the beginning of the end? Or something else entirely, that has nothing to do with beginnings or ends?

And, anyway, how can I assess all of this when I don't even know what I was trying to achieve in the first place? What was the point of this? Why did I meditate every day for a year?

Let's look at this logically. On the plus side: I'm still alive at the end of another year; I've meditated every day during that year and I've kept the longest journal I've ever managed to sustain in my life. These are all good things.

On the down side: twenty minutes is not long to meditate each day; I don't think I am any more enlightened at the end of the year compared to the start and I've no idea if this journal is of any interest or use to anyone.

All told, though, I'm pretty certain that my meditation project has been a good thing. Over the course of the year, I've enjoyed keeping this journal and it has touched on many themes with various relationships to meditation, Buddhism and daily practice. It has helped focus my thoughts.

It is, perhaps, this combination of modest meditation and journal-keeping that has produced the sole demonstrable effect of this project, which is that I have become more reflective. There are many signs of this, mainly related to improved awareness of my mental state at any given time and generally improved concentration and attentiveness.

For example, I used to be a voracious reader of books as a child and young adult, especially fiction, but this declined in my twenties and thirties as I focused more on work and writing research papers, articles and work-related books. Over the course of this past year, I have refound the inner quietude and concentration required to read more widely and in greater depth. I have not yet returned to fiction in a big way but I have increasingly read travel literature and other factual books. The key thing is: I now read more non-work-related material than I have over the past two decades. This is a good thing and I am much the better for it.

But will I continue to meditate every day after this year ends? Despite it being New Year's Eve, I resist the temptation to make a New Year's resolution about this. I've had enough of resolutions – so much for right resolve! I'll just wait and see how next year goes.

In January, I will write one final entry in this journal, with an update.

But for now, at the end of my year of daily meditation, I decide to eat some cake. I choose, of course, a slice of Christmas cake: fruitcake with marzipan on top and white icing on top of that again. This has been a staple of Christmas for many years for me and it is a richly nostalgic treat at the end of the day, the end of the month, the end of the year, the end of my meditation project.

And that is another thing that I have definitely learned this year: I really like cake.

NIRVANA

—

January

—

AN END TO SUFFERING?

I am sitting in a beautiful, high-ceilinged room, filled with light.

Again, it is the room that is filled with light; not me.

I try to meditate, but my mind keeps drifting to the past. For some reason I am reminded of a trip to Amsterdam. I went there with a friend for two nights. We ate wonderful Indonesian food on our first evening but on the second we were torn between two restaurants. He wanted to visit an Argentinian steakhouse but my eye was caught by a place a few doors away, painted psychedelic orange. It was a vegetarian café with a menu in multicoloured chalk and long-haired staff in tie-dyed clothes. I was smitten. Its name was Nirvana. My friend prevailed. We ate indifferent steaks and flew out of Amsterdam the following morning. I regretted our choice but soon forgot about it.

A year or so later, I started the daily meditation project documented in this journal. During that year, I read more about Buddhism than I had for a long time. I read about the four noble truths, the noble eight-fold path, various meditation practices and the meaning of *nirvana*. I was again enchanted by the depth and wisdom of Buddhist thought.

Nirvana is the end of suffering (*duhkha*). *Duhkha* or unsatisfactoriness is everywhere; this is the first noble truth of Buddhism (discussed in my journal in January). The second noble truth is the causes of *duhkha*: craving, hatred and delusion (February). The third is the cessation of suffering, achieved by facing *duhkha* and overcoming craving, aversion and delusion (March). This is the ultimate aim of Buddhist practice, *nirvana*.

The fourth noble truth (April) is how to overcome *duhkha* and attain *nirvana* through the noble eightfold path, based on the three key principles of wisdom, moral virtue and meditation. The eightfold path comprises right view (May), right resolve (June), right speech (July), right action (August), right livelihood (September), right effort (October), right mindfulness (November) and right concentration (December).

The path is non-linear. These eight factors do not form a sequence; they are all simultaneously relevant and each links with the others in profound, important ways. Together, they form a perfect whole. These eight factors reflect different facets of a unified approach to life that is centred on mindful awareness, wisdom and kindness, resulting in *nirvana*.

Many seek *nirvana* in Amsterdam. Perhaps some find it there. When I returned to Amsterdam in late November last year en route to India, I travelled with a colleague to a series of meetings with other psychiatrists. But I also found time to go in search of Nirvana, the vegetarian restaurant that had caught my eye some years earlier. I found no trace of Nirvana on the internet and, when I revisited the street, found the indifferent steakhouse immediately. But Nirvana had vanished. I had missed my chance.

Buddhism teaches that you never miss your chance. No matter what occurs in life, it passes. You pick up the pieces and you carry on. No matter what distractions arise and how you deal with them, you still have opportunity to just sit. This sounds deceptively simple. But the simplicity of this approach belies its challenges. It is incredibly difficult to let go of attachment and simply let things pass. It is difficult to just sit.

Just sitting and other meditative practices are, however, essential elements of Buddhism. Mindfulness is another important feature. Nowadays, it is easy to be cynical about meditation and mindfulness. Mindfulness in particular is everywhere, and often presented as the solution to everything from backache to unhappiness, poor eating habits to problems with parenting.

And, in a sense, it is. Many people already use some form of mindfulness without labelling it as such. I remember meeting a woman who loved to knit. She would sit for hours and hours, utterly absorbed in the rhythm of her needles. The rest of the world might as well not exist when she was knitting, once she was in the zone. She told me there was nothing in her head while she knitted, 'nothing at all'. When she heard about mindfulness, she said that knitting was exactly the same as mindfulness, just with a different name. And knitting, she added, was even better than mindfulness because with knitting you not only have a period of utter absorption in the present moment but you also end up with a lovely jumper.

Runners describe something similar (apart from the jumper): getting in the zone, attaining calm and feeling disciplined, happy and free. My own short-lived, ill-fated running efforts crop up from time to time in my journal. The less said about these efforts, the better.

But no single method suits everyone. For some people it is useful to label a specific activity as 'mindfulness' in order to focus their thoughts on what they are doing (or not doing) during a given period. For others, the label of 'mindfulness' is not helpful and even feels pretentious. So be it. One size does not fit all.

But it is meditation, clearly labelled as such, that has always attracted me, despite the various difficulties I encounter with practising it on a substantive, regular basis. That is what this journal has been about: figuring out why daily meditation is so hard, what we can do about it, and how to keep it going. In the next and final section of this book, I give advice on how to meditate.

It is often said that the purpose of meditation is not to have a good meditation sit, but to see the effects of meditation in your life between meditation sits. The aim of the practice is not to sit without distraction for twenty minutes or an hour, but to experience and overcome distraction and thus increase equanimity, flexibility, kindness, compassion, contentedness, reflectiveness and happiness between sessions. After all, even a master meditator spends most of their life not meditating but sleeping, eating, doing chores, checking emails and so forth. Meditation aims to make these times between meditation sits more skilful, reflective, fulfilling and enlightened.

So, did my year of daily meditation change my life? There are many answers to this question. In the first place, there was much about my life that was always unlikely to change as a result of meditation: where I live, what I work at and other aspects of my general situation. I did not want to change most of this anyway. While Buddha physically left his family and home to travel in search of truth, he did this *before* he was enlightened. There is nothing skilful or enlightened about abandoning others, reneging on commitments, or acting irresponsibly. As soon as he was enlightened, Buddha reached out to others again.

In any case, the story of Buddha is, at heart, a parable that demonstrates the importance of shedding old habits and building new ones that are more conducive to contemplation, compassion and happiness. And for me, the parts of my life that remained unchanged by my year of meditation were far greater than the parts that changed. That was to be expected: I wasn't looking for a revolution, but incremental, sustainable change.

But what did change, and how?

In my journal in December I concluded that I had become more reflective over the course of the year, as evidenced by enhanced awareness of my mental states (and their impermanence) and improved concentration and attentiveness. In particular, I refound the quietude and concentration required to read more widely. This is a really splendid, sustained development and it seems to reflect a greater ability to just sit and read. Of course, just sitting and reading is not quite the same as just sitting but it is surely better than constantly hopping around the place trying to do too many things at once and succeeding in none of them.

The other lesson I learned during my year of meditation is a rather counterintuitive one, especially for anyone who has binged on meditation handbooks over the years. Such books usually warn rather sternly about dealing with thoughts that intrude during meditation by letting them float past and not engaging with them in the slightest, resulting in their disappearance. What I found over the course of the year was that many of the thoughts that intrude during meditation are not frivolous or intrinsically undesirable. On the contrary, they are often important and relevant, and some are quite urgent. Of course, there are also many absurd, frivolous, repetitive and even obsessional thoughts, but a significant minority of intruding thoughts are actually important, not at all undesirable, and need to be dealt with.

This feature is evident in the many journal entries where I write about my work as a psychiatrist, mental illness, human rights, mental health legislation and other themes that routinely intrude in my head as I try to sit. These are not frivolous or insubstantial matters: they are key elements of who I am. And sometimes I remember quite important things that I might even jot down before resuming meditating.

The key skill that meditation teaches is to regulate these thoughts and thinking patterns, so as to reduce the likelihood of thoughts popping into one's head just as one is trying to clear the mind. Of course, once thoughts appear, one needs a strategy to deal with them, such as not responding unless there is a compelling case for doing so. This is not an easy skill to develop and it requires discipline. There is a good reason why meditation is described as a *practice*. We are always just practising.

So, apart from improved awareness of my mental states, increased concentration and realising that not quite all of my intrusive thoughts are entirely daft, did my year of daily meditation produce any other demonstrable results? Perhaps the most surprising for me is the final result: that I managed to keep this journal for a full twelve months. I will admit that I sometimes fell behind, but I always caught up quickly, with the result that the journal is a more-or-less contemporaneous account of the year. For better or worse, 2017 is now the most exhaustively documented year of my life.

And, finally, the biggest question of all: will I continue to meditate? Realistically, it is unlikely that I will remain a daily meditator. But I will meditate from time to time, hopefully quite frequently. I might even try harder to go on a meditation retreat at some point.

One of the interesting features of the past year was that while I got into the habit of daily meditation, I didn't go away to meditate in a sustained fashion for a couple of days or a weekend, as many people do. My three-night visit to a monastery in September was a general (and alarmingly literal) retreat from the world, rather than a meditation retreat. My time in India was spent in hotels rather than meditation centres. Perhaps that is something for me to work on in the new year? Longer periods of dedicated meditation? A retreat?

For now, though, my ambitions remain modest. I am not continuing this journal after this entry, and neither am I promising to meditate every day for the rest of my life. I will take it day by day.

HOW TO MEDITATE

—

There are thousands of guides to meditation available online and in various books, apps and manuals. Many are excellent. Some are useful. Others are just ridiculous. Overall, there are strong consistencies across the majority of sensible guidelines, reflecting relatively steady core values in meditation across different settings, different cultures and different spiritual traditions.

Some of the available guidelines are highly prescriptive, with rigid lists of dos and don'ts. Others are more flexible. The best guidelines provide advice that is specific enough to help most people with meditation but general enough to allow you to adopt the guidance to your own personality, circumstances and stage of practice.

What follows is a guide to meditation, based on my year of daily meditation. If you are doing the precise opposite of everything I say, and if your meditation is going well, ignore my advice. Simply continue doing what you're doing. But if you are struggling to meditate or feel oppressed by rigid guidelines, then it's worth looking afresh at how you are going about meditating. Meditation is not a punishment. It should not be something you 'fail' at. It should not be something you dread. Meditation should be something you look forward to, a welcoming space, an increasingly settled time.

Meditation is a 'practice' so there is always scope for improvement. The advice you need will vary over time, and hopefully this advice will help you at some point on your travels.

» Commit to meditate today (and only today)
Commit today to meditate today. That is, commit to meditating *on this day*. It is not necessary to commit to meditating tomorrow or to meditating every day for a week, a month, or a year (as I

did, possibly foolishly). Commitment beyond today just increases the pressure you place on yourself. It makes it more likely that you will abandon the project immediately: 'Why should I meditate today when I won't have the opportunity to meditate tomorrow, or for the rest of the week?'

Overcommitment is a recipe for procrastination. If you have the opportunity to meditate today, meditate today. Do not worry about tomorrow. Tomorrow will come in due course. And if you have the opportunity to meditate tomorrow, meditate tomorrow.

But today, just focus on today. Today is enough for now. Tomorrow will look after itself.

» Sit however you wish (there are no absolute rules)

We often think of meditators as sitting in the lotus position in a state of advanced renunciation and bliss. Or possibly levitating slightly, hovering a foot or so above the ground, suspended in mid-air by mixture of spiritual excellence, mystical insight and general transcendence.

Nothing could be further from the truth. There are thousands of meditation postures in use around the world. You just need to find one that suits you. If none of the described positions suits you, simply make one up.

There are some guidelines. In general terms, it is important that your body is straight and relaxed, your spine upright and you have a sense of stability and groundedness. For many people in the western world, this means sitting in a sturdy chair, both feet planted firmly on the floor and arms on the armrests or resting lightly on your knees, fingers touching gently.

The important thing is that you feel stable and grounded, upright and strong. You should settle on a position that you can sustain without undue discomfort or pain. Lying down is a bad idea: many people simply fall asleep. This is not necessarily a bad thing (sleep is good) but meditation requires relaxed awareness rather than somnolence. Sit in such a way as to make this possible for you.

Sit in a quiet place. I find music and other noises unhelpful but I do not obsess about finding absolute silence. You'll never find it. Just find a space away from the hustle and bustle of everyday life. There will still be sounds: cars passing, clocks ticking, birds singing, your stomach gurgling. Just note the sounds, let them pass and allow your mind to settle.

» Let your mind become clear

Clearing your mind is described as both a technique and a goal of meditation. But once you try to clear your mind, it fills immediately with a dozen different thoughts, all competing for attention. The best way to dispel this cluttered clamour is to try to detach from your mind and view it as if you are an observer looking through a telescope from outer space.

Better yet, do not think of this as 'clearing your mind' (which sounds very active) but rather 'letting your mind become clear' (considerably less active). Our minds are naturally clear and translucent. That is their natural resting state. If we let our minds settle down on their own, they will return to that state: clear as crystal and calm as the quietest sea.

The key is not to focus obsessively on anything in particular but rather to let intrusive thoughts drift away out of your mind. If you don't engage with your thoughts, they will vanish. This is not an active pushing away of thoughts but rather a decision not to engage, a decision to resist distraction and to let your mind settle at its own pace, in its own way. You cannot rush this but you can stand back and let it happen. Do so.

Developing this kind of self-awareness lies at the heart of meditative practice. Detaching from one's thoughts is difficult but becomes liberating as you get better at it. So much of what we think does not matter in the slightest. Let it go.

» Do not be upset if your mind remains cluttered

Notwithstanding my advice about letting your mind become clear, you won't manage to do it most of the time. Nobody does. This is precisely why you are meditating. If you were able to sit in a state of pure mental clarity, you would not need to practise meditation!

But like most people, you will probably experience intrusive thoughts as you try to let your mind become clear. Irritation and annoyance are natural but unhelpful responses in this situation. These responses feed into a vicious cycle: intrusive thoughts make you irritated and annoyed, being irritated and annoyed makes you feel like a failure at meditation, then you become more irritated and annoyed and so forth.

In these moments, it is useful to think of the simplest, best advice of all: just sit. Don't think, don't become annoyed, don't focus on anything. Just sit.

You will probably manage to just sit for a little while and will then get distracted by more intrusive thoughts. Don't worry. Let the thoughts or feelings come and then let them go. Let your irritation and annoyance come and go too. Just sit. Just sit. Just sit.

» Calm and insight

Traditionally, there are specific meditative practices aimed explicitly at attaining calmness (for example, mindfulness meditations) and specific practices aimed at attaining insight or wisdom (for example, Vipassanā). There are elaborate schemes for both kinds of meditation available online and elsewhere. But always start each meditation session with a simple, achievable exercise, like a 'body scan'.

The aim of the body scan is to centre you in the moment and in your body. Once you are seated comfortably in a relatively quiet spot, focus your mind on the top of your head and what it is feeling right now: hot, cold, tired, heavy, calm. Then work your way down your body with your mind, focusing on your neck, your chest, your arms and so forth, until your focused awareness finally reaches your toes. Feel each part of your body with your mind, not seeking to change anything but simply noting how your body feels right now, in this place, at this time.

Another good meditation to attain calmness is called 'the mindfulness of breathing'. For this practice, you focus on your breath, because it helps you ignore other thoughts that might arise and because your breath is always there. Having calmed your body gently and centred your thoughts in the moment, count each breath in your mind. First, count ten breaths on the in breath. Do not breathe especially quickly, slowly or deeply. Just breathe normally. Then count ten breaths on the out breath. And then count ten breaths on the turning of the breath. And then start again.

It is difficult to complete this exercise without getting distracted by intrusive thoughts or feelings, or becoming obsessed by the counting. The purpose of counting is simply to keep your mind alive to the moment and undistracted by anything other than your breath. Do not obsess about the counting. And if your mind drifts, just carry on from where you left off, after you let the distraction gently subside.

You can also try a 'loving kindness' meditation, which is a popular practice in meditation classes. First, calm your body (possibly with a body scan) and focus on the moment. Then spend a few minutes trying to feel loving kindness for yourself. Not just thinking about loving kindness; actually *feeling* it. Next, try to feel loving kindness for someone for whom it is easy to feel loving kindness (for example, a family member or friend you like). Then try to feel loving kindness for someone neutral (for example, a random person you saw in a shop earlier). After a little while, try to feel loving kindness for someone for whom you find it difficult to feel loving kindness (for example, someone who annoys you at work). Finish by trying to feel loving kindness for the whole world and all living beings in it.

With all these exercises, be gentle and kind to yourself.

Focus is difficult. This is the skill you are practising, so you will not be perfect. Forgive yourself. Start again.

Above all, do not castigate yourself for becoming distracted or even giving up on meditation for the day! Simply be aware that having difficulties means that there is more scope for you to improve and to benefit from the practice. Getting distracted and bringing your thoughts back to meditation *is* the work of meditation. That is what it's all about. That is the skill of meditating: training your mind to focus your attention on the present moment.

Resolve to do better tomorrow. If you sat for only three minutes today, aim for four minutes tomorrow or by next week. Be gentle with yourself, make your practice sustainable, and always remember to *just sit*.

» Practice makes better (if not perfect)

Aim to improve. If you meditate well this week, aspire to meditate better or more next week. Aim for sustainable, incremental progress. Do not aim for perfection, enlightenment or levitation. These will come in good time, I'm told.

For now, your aim is to improve day by day, week by week, year by year. Nothing more than this. You aim to practise. You aim to improve.

It is easy to lose hope with meditation, especially (and paradoxically) when you start to improve and when you start to look forward to meditating. After a good session, the world can seem loud and annoying, and it can seem as if your meditation sit brought no benefit, just irritation. This is 'post-meditation irritability' and it is very common.

If you experience this, remind yourself that the purpose of meditation is not to have a good meditation session. The purpose of meditation is to change your life. It is certainly good if you enjoy meditating but it is far better if you can see the effects of meditation in your life between meditation sits. If you are meditating well you will invariably become less impulsive in your day-to-day life, less likely to fly off the handle in the face of life's minor setbacks, more reflective and self-aware and more likely to live in the moment.

And in the end, that is all that matters: living in the moment. That is the purpose of meditation: to make us alive to the moment. This moment is all we have. It is all we will ever have. Life is a series of nows. We need to live them.

REFERENCES AND RECOMMENDED READING

–

These are the key references used in this book. Books and articles that are particularly recommended as general reading about meditation, mindfulness and Buddhism are highlighted in bold.

American Psychiatric Association. *Diagnostic and Statistical Manual of Mental Disorders (Fifth Edition)*. Arlington, VA: American Psychiatric Association, 2013.

Armstrong, K. *Buddha*. London: Phoenix, 2002.

Austin, J.H. *Zen and the Brain: Towards an Understanding of Meditation and Consciousness*. Cambridge, MA: MIT Press, 1999.

Austin, J.H. *Zen-Brain Reflections: Reviewing Recent Developments in Meditation and States of Consciousness*. Cambridge, MA: MIT Press, 2006.

Barry, S. *The Secret Scripture*. London: Faber and Faber Limited, 2008.

Batchelor, S. *Buddhism Without Beliefs: A Contemporary Guide to Awakening*. London: Bloomsbury, 1998.

Bechert, H. 'Buddhist revival in East and West'. In: Bechert, H. and Gombrich, R. (eds), *The World of Buddhism* (pp. 273–85). London: Thames & Hudson Ltd, 1984.

Bechert, H. and Gombrich, R. (eds). *The World of Buddhism*. London: Thames & Hudson Ltd, 1984.

Beckett, S. *Molloy*. Paris: Les Éditions de Minuit, 1947.

Beckett, S. *Malone Meurt*. Paris: Les Éditions de Minuit, 1951.

Beckett, S. *The Unnamable*. Paris: Les Éditions de Minuit, 1953.

Bellamy, C.D., Jarrett, N.C., Mowbray, O., McFarlane, P., Mowbray, C.T. and Holter, M.C. 'Relevance of spirituality for people with mental illness attending consumer-centred services'. *Psychiatric Rehabilitation Journal* 2007; 30: 287–94.

Bodhi, B. (ed.). *Abhidhammattha Sangaha: A Comprehensive Manual of Abhidhamma: The Philosophical Psychology of Buddhism*. Seattle, WA: BPS Pariyatti Editions, 1999.

Brazier, C. *Buddhist Psychology: Liberate Your Mind, Embrace Life*. London: Constable & Robinson Ltd, 2003.

Brennan, D. *Irish Insanity, 1800-2000*. Abingdon, Oxon.: Routledge, 2014.

Calvino, I. *Six Memos for the Next Millennium*. Cambridge, MA: Harvard University Press, 1988.

Cox, L. *Buddhism and Ireland: From the Celts to the Counter-Culture and Beyond*. Sheffield & Bristol, CT: Equinox, 2013.

Das, L.S. *Awakening the Buddha Within: Tibetan Wisdom for the Western World*. London: Bantam, 1997.

Davidson, R.J., Kabat-Zinn, J., Schumacher, J., Rosenkranz, M., Muller, D., Santorelli, S.F., Urbanowski, F., Harrington, A., Bonus, K. and Sheridan, J.F. 'Alterations in brain and immune function produced by mindfulness meditation'. *Psychosomatic Medicine* 2003; 65: 564–70.

Duffy, R.M. and Kelly, B.D. 'Concordance of the Indian Mental Healthcare Act 2017 with the World Health Organization's Checklist on Mental Health Legislation'. *International Journal of Mental Health Systems* 2017; 11: 48.

Eco, U. *The Name of the Rose*. New York, NY: Harcourt, 1983.

Epstein, M. *Thoughts Without a Thinker: Psychotherapy from a Buddhist Perspective*. New York, NY: Basic Books, 1995.

Epstein, M. *Psychotherapy Without the Self: A Buddhist Perspective*. New Haven & London: Yale University Press, 2007.

Freud, S. *Jokes and Their Relation to the Unconscious*. London: Hogarth Press, 1960.

Fromm, E., Suzuki, D. and Demartino, R. *Zen Buddhism and Psychoanalysis*. New York, NY: Harper & Row, 1960.

Gethin, R. *The Foundations of Buddhism.* Oxford and New York, NY: Oxford University Press, 1998.

Gopnik, A. 'American Nirvana'. *The New Yorker* 2017; 7 and 14 August.

Greally, H. *Bird's Nest Soup.* Dublin: Allen Figgis & Co., 1971.

Harvey, P. *An Introduction to Buddhism: Teachings, History and Practices.* Cambridge: Cambridge University Press, 1990.

Hesse, H. *Siddhartha.* London: Penguin, 2003.

Holtz, T.H. 'Refugee trauma versus torture trauma: A retrospective controlled cohort study of Tibetan refugees'. *Journal of Nervous and Mental Diseases* 1998; 186; 24–34.

Holtz, T.H. *A Doctor in Little Lhasa: One Year in Dharamsala with the Tibetans in Exile.* Indianapolis, IN: Dog Ear Publishing, 2009.

Houshmand, Z., Livingston, R.B. and Wallace, B.A. (eds). *Consciousness at the Crossroads: Conversations with the Dalai Lama on Brain Science and Buddhism.* Ithaca, NY: Snow Lion, 1999.

Iyer, P. *The Lady and the Monk: Four Seasons in Kyoto.* New York, NY: Alfred A. Knopf, 1991.

Iyer, P. *The Open Road: The Global Journey of the Fourteenth Dalai Lama.* New York, NY: Alfred A. Knopf, 2008.

Joyce, J. *Ulysses.* Paris: Shakespeare and Company, 1922.

Joyce, J. *Finnegans Wake.* London: Faber and Faber Limited, 1939.

Kabat-Zinn, J. *Wherever You Go, There You Are: Mindfulness Meditation for Everyday Life.* New York, NY: Hyperion, 1994.

Kabat-Zinn, J., Massion, A.O., Kristeller, J., Peterson, L.G., Fletcher, K.E., Pbert, L., Lenderking, W.R. and Santorelli, S.F. 'Effectiveness of a meditation-based stress reduction program in the treatment of anxiety disorders'. *American Journal of Psychiatry* 1992; 149: 936–43.

Kelly, B.D. 'Medical romance'. *Lancet* 2007; 370: 1482.

Kelly, B.D. 'Meditation, mindfulness and mental health'. *Irish Journal of Psychological Medicine* 2008; 25: 3–4.

Kelly, B.D. 'Buddhist psychology, psychotherapy and the brain: A critical introduction'. *Transcultural Psychiatry* 2008; 45: 5–30.

Kelly, B.D. 'Recovered memories of past lives: Psychology, philosophy and spirituality'. *Irish Psychiatrist* 2009; 4: 227–32.

Kelly, B.D. 'Highlighting the plight of refugees'. *Irish Medical Times* 2009; 10 July.

Kelly, B.D. 'Self-immolation and suicide'. *Irish Psychiatrist* 2011; 12: 133–4.

Kelly, B.D. 'Self-immolation, suicide and self-harm in Buddhist and western traditions'. *Transcultural Psychiatry* 2011; 48: 299–317.

Kelly, B.D. 'Contemplative traditions and meditation'. In: Miller, L. (ed.), *Oxford Handbook of Psychology and Spirituality* (pp. 307–25). Oxford: Oxford University Press, 2012.

Kelly, B.D. 'Mental health need amongst the intellectually disabled'. *Irish Journal of Medical Science* 2013; 182: 539.

Kelly, B.D. 'DSM-5 - Plus ça change, plus c'est la même chose?' *Irish Medical Times* 2013; 27 September.

Kelly, B.D. 'Compassion, cognition and the illusion of self: Buddhist notes towards more skilful engagement with diagnostic classification systems in psychiatry'. In: Shonin, E., Van Gordon, W. and Griffiths, M.D. (eds), *Mindfulness* and *Buddhist-Derived Approaches in Mental Health and Addiction* (pp. 9–28). Heidelberg: Springer, 2015.

Kelly, B.D. *Hearing Voices: The History of Psychiatry in Ireland.* Dublin: Irish Academic Press, 2016.

Kelly, B.D. 'Medical romance: Love never dies'. *Lancet* 2016; 388: 2989.

Kelly, B.D. 'Mental health, mental illness, and human rights in India and elsewhere: What are we aiming for?' *Indian Journal of Psychiatry* 2016; 58 (suppl. 2): S168-S174.

Kelly, B.D. *Mental Health in Ireland: The Complete Guide for Patients, Families, Health Care Professionals and Everyone Who Wants To Be Well.* Dublin: The Liffey Press, 2017.

Kelly, B.D. 'Ego, id and Ireland'. *Lancet Psychiatry* 2017; 4: 281–2.

Kelly, B.D. 'How we define Buddhism'. *The New Yorker* 2017; 4 September.

Kelly, B.D. 'A case of hysteria, three essays on sexuality and other works'. *Irish Medical Times* 2017; 20 January.

Kelly, B.D. 'The Freud project, year eight: jokes and the unconscious'. *Irish Medical Times* 2018; 13 April.

Kornfield, J. *After the Ecstasy, the Laundry: How the Heart Grows Wise on the Spiritual Path.* New York, NY: Bantam Books, 2000.

Krakauer, J. 'Death of an innocent'. *Outside* 1993; January.

Krakauer, J. *Into the Wild.* New York, NY: Villard Books, 1995.

Krisanaprakornkit, T., Krisanaprakornkit, W., Piyavhatkul, N. and Laopaiboon, M. 'Meditation therapy for anxiety disorders'. *Cochrane Database of Systematic Reviews* 2006; 1:CD004998.

Krisanaprakornkit, T., Witoonchart, C. and Krisanaprakornkit, W. 'Meditation therapies for attention deficit / hyperactivity disorder (protocol)'. *Cochrane Database of Systematic Reviews* 2007; 2: CD006507.

Kvaerne, P. 'Tibet: The rise and fall of a monastic tradition'. In: Bechert, H. and Gombrich, R. (eds), *The World of Buddhism* (pp. 253–70). London: Thames & Hudson Ltd, 1984.

Layard, R. *Happiness: Lessons from a New Science.* London: Penguin, 2005.

Leidy, D.P. *The Art of Buddhism: An Introduction to its History and Meaning.* Boston & London: Shambhala Publications, Inc., 2008.

Leskov, N. *Lady Macbeth of the Mtsensk District and Other Stories.* London: Penguin Classics, 2015 (original work: 1865).

Lutz, A., Greischar, L.L., Rawlings, N.B., Ricard, M. and Davidson, R.J. 'Long-term meditators self-induce high-amplitude gamma synchrony during mental practice'. *Proceedings of the National Academy of Sciences of the United States of America* 2004; 101: 16369-73.

McLeod, M. (ed.). *Mindful Politics: A Buddhist Guide to Making the World a Better Place.* Boston: Wisdom Publications, 2006.

McQuaid, J.C. 'Introduction'. In: O'Doherty, E.F. and McGrath, S.D. (eds), *The Priest and Mental Health* (pp. ix–xi). New York, NY: Alba House, 1963.

Melvin-Koushki, M. 'Imperial talismanic love: Ibn Turka's *Debate of Feast and Fight* (1426) as philosophical romance and lettrist mirror for Timurid princes'. *Der Islam* 2019; 96: 1 (forthcoming).

Merton, T. *The Seven Storey Mountain.* New York, NY: Harcourt, Brace and Company, 1948.

Michie, D. *The Dalai Lama's Cat.* London: Hay House UK Ltd, 2012.

Morris, J. *Conundrum*. London: Faber and Faber Limited, 1974.

Morrison Welsh, A. and Hollyday, J. *Held in the Light: Norman Morrison's Sacrifice for Peace and His Family's Journey of Healing*. New York, NY: Orbis Books, 2008.

Mühling, J. *A Journey into Russia*. London: The Armchair Traveller at the bookHaus, 2014.

Newberg, A., Pourdehnad, M., Alavi, A. and d'Aquili, E.G. 'Cerebral blood flow during meditative prayer: Preliminary findings and methodological issues'. *Perceptual and Motor Skills* 2003; 97: 625–30.

Nichtern, E. *One City: A Declaration of Interdependence*. Boston: Wisdom Publications, 2007.

Nyanaponika, T. *Heart of Buddhist Meditation*. Newburyport, MA: Red Wheel/Weiser, 1976.

Nyanaponika, T. *Abhidhamma Studies: Buddhist Explorations of Consciousness and Time (Fourth Edition)*. Boston, MA: Wisdom Press, 1998.

O'Halloran, M. *Pure Heart, Enlightened Mind*. Boston, MA: Charles E. Tuttle Co., Inc., 1994 (Boston, MA: Wisdom Publications, 2007).

Parks, T. *Teach Us to Sit Still: A Sceptic's Search for Health and Healing*. London: Harvill Secker, 2010.

Pearsall, J. and Trumble, B. (eds). *The Oxford English Reference Dictionary (Second Edition)*. Oxford: Oxford University Press, 1996.

Plath, S. *The Bell Jar*. London: William Heinemann, 1963.

Reuters. 'Buddhists free lobsters to live another day'. *Guardian* 2011; 5 August.

Ryan, T. *A Mindful Nation: How a Simple Practice Can Help Us Reduce Stress, Improve Performance, and Recapture the American Spirit*. Carlsbad, CA: Hay House, 2012.

Sephton, S.E., Salmon, P., Weissbecker, I., Ulmer, C., Floyd, A., Hoover, K. and Studts, J.L. 'Mindfulness meditation alleviates depressive symptoms in women with fibromyalgia: Results of a randomised clinical trial'. *Arthritis and Rheumatism* 2007; 57: 77–85.

Shields, C. *Unless*. London: Fourth Estate/HarperCollins, 2002.

Shloss, C.L. *Lucia Joyce: To Dance in the Wake*. London: Bloomsbury, 2004.

Sogyal, R. *The Tibetan Book of Living and Dying*. New York, NY: HarperCollins, 1992.

Tanahashi, K. 'Four truths and ten laws'. In: McLeod, M. (ed.), *Mindful Politics: A Buddhist Guide to Making the World a Better Place* (pp. 301–2). Boston, MA: Wisdom Publications, 2006.

Thoreau, H.D. *Walden or Life in the Woods*. Boston, MA: Ticknor and Fields, 1854.

Trungpa, C. *Glimpses of Abhidharma*. London: Shambhala, 2001.

Tucker, M.E. and Williams, D.R. (eds). *Buddhism and Ecology: The Interconnection of Dharma and Deeds*. Cambridge, MA: Harvard University Press, for the Harvard University Center for the Study of World Religions, 1997.

Turner, A., Cox, L. and Bocking, B. (eds). 'Special Issue: U Dhammaloka, "The Irish Buddhist": Rewriting the History of Early Western Buddhist Monastics'. *Contemporary Buddhism: An Interdisciplinary Journal* 2010; 11: 121–291.

Vance, J.D. *Hillbilly Elegy: A Memoir of a Family and Culture in Crisis*. London: William Collins, 2016.

Wachholtz, A.B. and Pargament, K.I. 'Is spirituality a critical ingredient of meditation? Comparing the effects of spiritual meditation, secular meditation and relaxation on spiritual, psychological, cardiac and pain outcomes'. *Journal of Behavioral Medicine* 2005; 28: 69–84.

Woeser, T. *Immolations au Tibet: La Honte du Monde.* Montpellier: Indigène Éditions, 2013.

Woeser, T. *Tibet on Fire: Self-Immolations Against Chinese Rule.* London and New York, NY: Verso, 2016.

World Health Organization. *The ICD-10 Classification of Mental and Behavioural Disorders: Clinical Descriptions and Diagnostic Guidelines.* Geneva: World Health Organization, 1992.

Acknowledgements

—

I am very grateful to everyone who assisted me as I wrote this book. I deeply appreciate the support of my wife, Regina, and children, Eoin and Isabel. I am also very grateful to my parents, Mary and Desmond; sisters, Sinéad and Niamh; and nieces, Aoife and Aisling. Trixie also deserves special mention: Hi, Trixie!

I owe a long-standing debt of gratitude to my teachers at Scoil Chaitríona, Renmore, Galway; St Joseph's Patrician College, Nun's Island, Galway; and the School of Medicine at NUI Galway. I am also very grateful to Dr Larkin Feeney, Dr John Bruzzi, Mr Len Harrow, Mr Eoghan Marrow, Dr Séamus Mac Suibhne, Mr David Givens, Ms Vanessa Fox O'Loughlin, everyone at Gill Books, my extraordinary work colleagues, my patients, their families and many, many others.

Permissions

—

Material adapted from the *Irish Medical Times* is reproduced by kind permission of the *Irish Medical Times*. Material adapted from *Irish Psychiatrist* is reproduced by kind permission of MedMedia Group.

'Meditation, Mindfulness and Mental Health' (adapted for this book) was originally published as: Kelly, B.D. Meditation, mindfulness and mental health. *Irish Journal of Psychological Medicine* 2008; 25(1): 3-4. doi: 10.1017/S0790966700010752 © Cambridge University Press 2008, published by Cambridge University Press. Reprinted with permission, and with the agreement of MedMedia Group and the College of Psychiatrists of Ireland.

'Ego, id and Ireland' is reprinted from *The Lancet Psychiatry*, 4(4), B.D. Kelly, 'Ego, id and Ireland', pages 281–2, © 2017, with permission from Elsevier.

I am very grateful to the editors, publishers, authors and copyright holders who permitted reuse of material in this book. All reasonable efforts have been made to contact the copyright holders for all material used. If any have been omitted, please contact the publisher.